# CHRISTIAN CREATIVITY

## How to Make Money With Your God-Given Gift

Butch Hartman

*Christian Creativity*

*DEDICATION:*

*I want to dedicate this book to my amazing wife Julieann. She not only helps me keep my creativity burning at 100%, she also helped me create our two incredible daughters, Carly & Sophia – two of my greatest creations ever.*

# Contents

# A Word to the Creative Person

This book was once just a pile of blank pages. It was a completely vast open space brimming with possibilities and just waiting to be written upon. The blank pages had one thing going for them: potential.

But until someone sat down to create and place the words upon them, the pages would simply sit here, forever, as a blank, unrealized landscape. So would the potential. Sometimes, that's what we do: We leave things blank. We leave the potential on the table because we think we don't have the time, ability, or duty to fill up the blank pages with anything. Sometimes, as far as we're concerned, being creative is someone else's job.

That's where we're wrong: Being creative is OUR job. If you are a creative person, it's your job because you're filled with great purpose and potential.

Back to the blank pages.

When I began typing these words, the landscape of the pages began to slowly change. With each stroke of the keyboard, the world of blankness began to fill with thoughts, ideas, and visions. Pretty soon—after many days, weeks, and months mixed with a healthy dose of motivation—the landscape was finally finished, and here it is: a fully realized vision that was once only a bunch of random thoughts that would have remained unspoken and unrealized had I not typed them out.

The same goes for you. As creative as you may be, not one single person will ever know about your creativity until you begin making it a reality. Think of it this way as well: No one would have heard Jesus' message had He not bothered to take steps into society to deliver it, and we certainly would have not heard His message today had someone not written it down for future generations to read.

Your creativity is completely and totally at your disposal. All you have to do is apply yourself. This is the part where most of us get hung up. Sometimes, we don't know HOW to apply ourselves. Yet it is a completely necessary step. But once you take that step, and then the next and the next, before you know it, your vision will become fully realized.

The timing is up to you. Just as God created the world, you can also create something. But remember: God was very purposeful and focused as He realized the vision that would ultimately become the earth and the reality we now find ourselves in. I'm not saying that any of us is God, but I am saying that we are created in His image, and as such, we have His same creative talents.

As a fellow creative, I am asking you—practically begging you—not to let your creativity go to waste. So many great things can come from it. Not only can you change your life with it, you can change the lives of those around you, maybe even the lives of the entire world. Steve Jobs, Leonardo DaVinci, Michael Jackson, or Walt Disney know something about that.

God created the universe, He created you in it, and He created the creativity within you. Seems like He had a reason for doing so and went to a lot of trouble to make YOU happen.

Now that He's made YOU happen, go make your vision happen. It's time. Fill up those blank pages.

**Butch Hartman**

October 2024

# Section 1: Inspiration

Your life could change today.

Yes. Today. Right now.

Why do I know this?

Because you have ideas, and ideas are valuable. You have an idea inside you that can change everything. It can change your life, your family's life, and the lives of future generations.

All you need to do is make one—or more—of those ideas into a reality.

Ready? Let's do this.

# Are You a Christian Creative?

*That if you confess with your mouth the Lord Jesus and believe in your heart that God has raised Him from the dead, you will be saved (Romans 10:9).*

If you've confessed Jesus and invited Him into your heart, then you're a Christian. There is no greater decision in life. I'm assuming you already know that since you've decided to read this book. You've made the greatest, life-altering choice a human being can make, and you're living life as a follower of the One True King. That's awesome! It shows that, though you may live in this world, you have realized that you are not OF this world (see John 17:14–15). You have decided to live life according to the King's terms and not the terms of the world system. This not only means that you'll go to Heaven when you leave this earth, but you can bring Heaven DOWN to earth as you live out your life—just like Jesus said when He taught us to pray:

*"Your will be done on earth as it is in heaven" (Matthew 6:10; Luke 11:2).*

But being a creative person is also an incredible thing, isn't it? So, combining the two and being a "creative Christian" or "Christian creative" should be the most amazing thing of all time, right?

After all, we serve a creative God. We're made in His image! Not only in the way He looks physically, but also the way He IS! If He's creative, then WE'RE creative, and no matter how much we may think we aren't, we ARE! He has given all His children gifts and talents to prosper them on the earth:

*He has filled them with skill to do all kinds of work as engravers, designers, embroiderers in blue, purple and scarlet yarn and fine linen, and weavers—all of them skilled workers and designers (Exodus 35:35 NIV).*

Creativity is a God-given gift. There are those who follow the Lord and believe they've been given an incredible gift by Him and are working to develop that gift every single day. Then there are those who may believe that they aren't creative. The enemy has lied to them their entire lives and told them that they have no creativity. Sadly, these individuals have bought into the lie "hook, line, and sinker." But that is what our adversary is very good at: lying. After all, he is the father of lies:

*"You are of your father the devil…. When he speaks a lie, he speaks from his own resources, for he is a liar and the father of it" (John 8:44).*

The last thing on earth the enemy wants is for you to understand just how powerful your creativity is. And that's exactly what creativity is: powerful. If creativity weren't, then the enemy wouldn't bother trying to take it from you. He comes to steal everything of any value because he can create nothing new on his own.

*"The thief comes only to steal and kill and destroy" (John 10:10 NIV).*

Your creativity is there, and you are most definitely aware of it. It's like a compulsion you can't get rid of. You know for a fact you're supposed to do something, but either you aren't sure about it or have been discouraged from it because of your own actions or the actions and words of others. Everyone understands that they have SOME creativity, but there are those who tap into it more easily than others do.

Perhaps life has happened in such a way that you've been forced to focus on things other than your creativity. Bills to pay, jobs to find, kids to feed, etc. We all understand how life can throw things at us very steadily and at the most inconvenient of times. We all know how our creativity can get buried underneath all the cares of the world. But your creativity is most definitely something that is yours and yours alone.

Think about that.

God gave YOU something that is ESPECIALLY for you and no one else! What a great heavenly Father we serve! And as Christians the desire of our hearts should be—first and foremost—to serve our heavenly Father. We want to glorify God in all we do, and through our creativity, we want to draw attention to Jesus and no one else!

*I praise you, for I am fearfully and wonderfully made. Wonderful are your works; my soul knows it very well (Psalm 139:14 ESV).*

*"Worthy are you, our Lord and God, to receive glory and honor and power, for you created all things, and by your will they existed and were created" (Revelation 4:11 ESV).*

Knowing you're creative is one thing. But knowing how to USE your creativity to glorify the Lord and—yes, this is very important—make a living, too, is what this book is all about. So, let's get going and learn how to access our God-given creativity so we can glorify the Lord in all we do. Let's use the power that God has given us and change the world.

And it all begins now. Ready?

Let's start first by having you write down some things about your creativity. (You'll soon notice I ask you to write things down a lot.) The Lord told the prophet Habakkuk:

*Write the vision and make it plain on tablets, that he may run who reads it (Habakkuk 2:2).*

You see, writing things down makes them more real, more tangible, and even more possible to us. God is a very big advocate of writing things down, isn't He? He wrote down the Ten Commandments for Moses. And we have the Bible we can turn to every day! If writing was good enough for God, it's good enough for us.

It's my desire to help you practice writing things down concerning your creativity, your ideas, next steps to take, etc., all with the hope of prompting you to begin to make your vision, your creativity, a reality. So, please take the time to do the interactive stuff, and we'll start right now by creating a list of your creative talents.

## List the Creative Talents You Have:

*If you need more space, then don't be afraid to write all over the pages of this book! Make them as "non-blank" as possible!*

1.

2.

3.

4.

5.

# It's Time to Wake Up

You've been asleep too long. Now, more than ever is the time to wake up.

*But I'm wide awake while I'm reading this book!* is what you're probably thinking.

That's not the kind of "waking up" I'm talking about. I don't mean waking up from a physical sleep. I'm talking about a SPIRITUAL wake up. Your creative spirit may have been dormant for a long time now. If it has been, then this is definitely the chapter for you.

A human being has three things: a mind, a soul, and a spirit. The spirit is the energy source that affects everything. Ever heard the phrase "broken-hearted"? The heart isn't physically broken, but the spirit is. When a spirit is broken or oppressed, the entire body begins to feel the effects. That can make us sad, depressed, or even physically ill. Sometimes, we've been broken-hearted so long that we just accept it as part of our lives. It becomes so familiar that we don't even see it anymore.

Well, it's time to start seeing it. The sooner we realize that our spirit needs to wake up, the sooner we can start pursuing our God-given calling.

Without a fire in your spirit, your creativity will always be put on the backburner. It's your spirit that fuels your creativity. If you're a creative person, then you should understand one key word: MOTIVATION. Motivation is what keeps us moving. It keeps us sailing against the wind. Keeps us looking over the horizon. But the thing about motivation is that it's completely our own responsibility to keep it fed. Without it, we slow down. We lag. We let the goal get farther and farther away. This is not the way to achieve; this is the way to lose and continue to lose.

There are many things in our lives that can cause us to lose motivation: family issues, job issues, bills, poor health, lack of results, to name a few. The fact that our dream hasn't come true overnight can make us think that God has forgotten all about us. "Lord, why hasn't this happened for me yet?" you may be asking Him. "Why does everything seem to be taking so long?" This is a very common string of questions for creative people who also happen to be Christians. Yet the great thing you have at your disposal as a Christian is the ultimate weapon: God's Word. Because even when things get in the way, we have our heavenly Father to turn to for encouragement and advice.

*"I tell you the truth, you can say to this mountain, 'May you be lifted up and thrown into the sea,' and it will happen. But you must really believe it will happen and have no doubt in your heart" (Mark 11:23 NLT).*

As Christians, we need to use our words creatively. Our words are powerful! God created the entire universe with His words. He said, "'Let there be light!'" and there was light" (Genesis 1:3). And if we are made in His image, then we have power in our words, too.

When your motivation seems to be lacking you MUST speak words of power and encouragement over yourself. "I am creative." "I am victorious." "I am filled with amazing ideas." These words and phrases may seem unusual to you at first, but they can be part of the energy that begins to reignite your motivation. Train yourself to become disciplined in the practice of speaking positively over yourself.

*Death and life are in the power of the tongue, and those who love it will eat its fruit (Proverbs 18:21).*

You alone can speak death or life to your dream. Others may speak negatively over you, but you can counteract their negative words with positive ones.

Hey, I just saved you a bunch of money. Now you don't have to go out and buy a "self-help" book. You have the greatest self-help book there is: the Bible!

Think of an Olympic athlete or a world-class musician. A great majority of their life and time has been spent practicing and practicing, getting out on the track or the ice rink or picking up their instrument day after day and working with it. Sometimes, it takes years, but guess what: That's what it takes. And the only way to get through the endless hours of what you're working on or working toward is to stay motivated.

So how do we do that? How do we awaken the fire inside and keep ourselves excited about our calling? We look at our lives and ask: "What motivates me, and what have I done to motivate myself in the past?" We want to think about ways that have worked before and even come up with new ways to inspire ourselves.

List Several Ways You Can Motivate Yourself:

1.

2.

3.

4.

5.

# Your Calling

God has empowered you to be creative, correct? But HOW are you going to put your creativity to good use? What are you supposed to do that will not only satisfy that creative impulse, but will glorify God in the process?

These are all good questions, but the real question you need to ask yourself is: What are YOU called to do?

What is it that excites you and gets you up in the morning? What special thing do you look forward to doing each and every day? God doesn't just want you doing it as a hobby. A hobby is something you do on the side that you *wish* you could do for a living. A CALLING is doing what you're meant to do—something you know is the thing you'll be remembered for.

Have you found your calling yet? And if so, where are you in the process of realizing it? Just beginning? Been doing it for a while? Or are you now fully immersed in it and even teaching others how to do it?

Think of your creativity as a seed. You plant it, you tend to it, it grows, then you reap a harvest.

But if you're a person who puts things off due to fear, doubt, laziness, or anything else, the calling will wait and wait and wait until someone else picks up the mantle and runs with it. Have you ever seen some successful person out there who's known for a great idea, and you say to yourself, *Man, I could have done that*?

My question is: Why didn't you?

Maybe the answer is you didn't know you were supposed to because you didn't know what your calling was in the first place. It's time to find out. It's time to move toward something even if the path is not completely illuminated for you.

This is called faith. You need faith in the Lord to show you each step along the way. People who don't believe in Jesus only have their wits, experience, emotions, and maybe the advice of others to show them the way, and we all know how untrustworthy and inconsistent those things can be, right?

But as Christians, we have our faith in Jesus and His promises that can show us the way. After all, He says that He's "the way, the truth, and the life" (John 14:6). What better example is there than He?

Learn your calling and step out in faith.

## List Several Possibilities of What Your Calling Could Be:

1.

2.

3.

# Should I Make Money as a Christian Creative?

So many of us Christians are taught that making money is wrong. After all, only selfish people are concerned about money, right? Christian people would never be into making money, would we? Fellow Christians often pull out this scripture to help us see the evil of money:

*The love of money is a root of all kinds of evil... (1 Timothy 6:10).*

But if we read that scripture carefully, it doesn't say MONEY is THE root of all evil. It says the LOVE of money is a root of all kinds of evil. The exaltation or worship of money is the cause or source of evil. When all we do is focus on money, then it becomes an idol to us. We begin to worship it. Idolizing anything over our Lord Jesus is wrong, and that includes idolizing money.

People routinely put money and material things above God, but that does not mean it's the right thing to do. In fact, the first commandment (of the famous Ten Commandments) says:

*"You shall have no other gods before Me" (Deuteronomy 5:6).*

That includes anything—money, fame, family, fleshly desires— anything that takes your attention away from God. I say all this to remind you that, as a Christian, you're working to further the Kingdom of God. Glorifying Him should be first and foremost in your mind.

*"Seek first the kingdom of God and His righteousness, and all these things shall be added unto you" (Matthew 6:33).*

That's what Christianity is all about. We pursue relationship with Jesus while the rest of the world pursues worldly possessions. And the Bible promises that, as we pursue Him, favor, blessings, and abundance will flow to us as a byproduct. Trust me, it's worked in my life, and it can work in yours, too.

Focus on growing in HIM through your gift and watch how He'll bless you *and* your gift. Jesus has no ego. He washed the disciples' feet (see John 13: 1—17).

This is not about blessing Him because He needs to feel better about Himself like any other person would. No. He wants you to glorify Him because He knows it is the best thing for YOU. Focusing your efforts, your purpose, and your mind on Him is beneficial for every aspect of your life. Remember that as you drive toward your goal.

So, is it okay to make money as a Christian? Absolutely! As long as you remember that you're working for Him and not the money. Jesus gave you your gift. Thank Him by dedicating your purpose and goals to Him. This is the difference between you and the rest of the world.

Making money as a Christian creative is absolutely 100 percent okay. Think of the amazing things you can do for the Kingdom once you become a money maker. You can even help others in many ways!

## List Some Things You Would Like to Do in the Kingdom of God once You Have Enough Money:

*Hey, if you want to list more go ahead!*

1.

2.

3.

4.

Let's continue to look at what the Bible says about making money.

> *"But remember the Lord your God, for it is He who gives you the ability to produce wealth, and so confirms his covenant, which he swore to your ancestors, as it is today" (Deuteronomy 8:18 NIV).*

It says He (the Lord) gives us the power or ability to generate wealth.

Do you think God would give us the power to produce wealth if He didn't want us to produce wealth? That's not really a hard question, is it?

But He doesn't just hand over the wealth. There would be no growth or faith involved in that. It would be like a rich kid getting money from his dad all the time. Yes, the rich kid would have money, but he would have no knowledge of how to make it himself or how to teach anyone else how to make money. In other words, the knowledge would die with the rich father, and the rich kid would starve without the dad. This is not a great formula for growth.

For us to grow and to multiply, we must learn and develop, not solely our physical bodies, but our skills and spirituality as well.

In Genesis 1:28, our Lord told Adam and Eve (and us vicariously) to "be fruitful and multiply." He didn't tell them or us to keep taking and do nothing to contribute. He is not that kind of God. To multiply, you must invest or plant something. To plant something, you must have something to plant. You can either plant for someone else (doing your regular job, the one where you receive a paycheck), or you can plant for yourself (having your own business). Either way, you're growing something, and growing anything takes creativity.

So, yes, you can absolutely use your creativity to make money as a Christian. And by the way, you can also feel good about it, too!

*Beloved, I pray that you may prosper in all things and be in health, just as your soul prospers (3 John 1:2).*

See? He wants us to prosper in ALL things, and that means in our creativity, too.

Let me say it again, but in a different way: Using your creativity to make a living is A-okay with God!

And why shouldn't you make money doing what you love? We are trained up as kids to conform to the idea that life is all about a 9 to 5 job, 5 days a week, 1 week of vacation, and retirement at age 65.

Do you see how this type of thinking can be limiting?

I'm not saying it's wrong or bad to live life this way, but I AM saying that life doesn't always have to be like that. Life can be whatever you make it out to be. Once again, you're in charge. You're in absolute complete control over the decisions you make. I know there may be life situations that make it more difficult to do certain things—for example, a person with a wife or husband and four kids can't just pick up and move to a new state as easily as a single, unmarried person with no kids—but things are doable if we have the desire and passion to do them.

So HOW do we make money by pursuing our vision? What exactly are the steps we need to take to be sure that our time and energy are used properly?

You've probably spent a lot of time thinking about this, and it seems very intimidating, right? Fear not because this book will really help answer some of your questions. For now, though, fill in the following worksheet to see exactly how you feel about making money with your God-given gifts and talents.

### Answer the Following Questions Related to How You Feel about Money:

1. Do you feel it's wrong to make money as a Christian creative? If so, why?

2. Have you ever wanted to make money as a Christian creative?

3. If you knew you could make money using your gifts would you do it?

4. Would you prefer to make money at a standard 9-5 job or by using your God-given gifts?

# Your Idea Could Change Your Life

Ever had a great idea? Of course you have. We all have.

Ever have more than one? More than two? More than three?

I'll bet you—like everyone else—have had about a million ideas. But it's the people that TELL others about their ideas that get their ideas to come to fruition. It's a fact: The best ideas usually take more than one person to make them a reality.

I know there's an insecurity that comes with sharing an idea. But it's the conquering of that fear of sharing that will enable us to make the idea a reality.

*Yet in all these things we are more than conquerors through Him who loved us (Romans 8:37).*

When I had the idea for *The Fairly Oddparents* back in October of 1997, I had two options: tell someone about it or NOT tell someone about it.

What would you have done?

Obviously, now that *The Fairly Oddparents* has become one of the most popular cartoons in the world and has made multiple hundreds of millions of dollars, you would hopefully say: "Yes! Of course I would have told EVERYONE about it!"

That's an easy one. WE already KNOW the cartoon is and continues to be a success. Easy to tell everyone how awesome it is and to get people to believe in it after the fact, right? Very little fear or faith involved in that.

But what about on day one—on day one of the idea, that is? Every idea EVER has a day one.

On day one, it is extremely hard to get anyone—sometimes, even yourself—to believe in the idea. It's just a fleeting thought. It's a dream. A hope. A fantasy.

All those descriptions, however, do not describe a reality.

A house. That's a reality. A shoe. Reality. A toothbrush. Reality. A car, an elevator, a phone, a hat, bucket, a pair of sunglasses—all reality.

But all of them started off as ideas. We could list 1,000 more, but you get the point: Someone somewhere, FOR THE FIRST TIME EVER, thought of each and every item I listed. There was a "day one" for each. But as important as a day one is for an idea, there is an even more important day.

Day two.

Yep. ANYONE can think of something, and they have. But do they—do YOU—have the courage and the desire to carry it on to a second day? A third? A fourth, fifth, etc.?

You see, it's the dedication—the commitment to the idea or the faith—that keeps us moving forward. The Bible says,

*Faith is the substance of things hoped for, the evidence of things not seen (Hebrews 11:1).*

It's the HOPE that will always motivate us, but we need to choose to follow that hope. That faith. Jesus always gives us options. He will never ever force us to do anything. It's all our own choice.

When faith is in the picture, we can trust ourselves to move forward even if what we are moving into is the unknown.

## Write Something You Can Do That Will Keep You Faithful to Your Idea:

*For example, you could write, "Make at least one phone call a day," or "Write down one new sales lead per day."*

1.

2.

3.

4.

5.

# Fear!

Time to admit it. This all seems to scare you. Maybe it doesn't provoke bone-chilling, horror movie terror, but it makes you nervous, doesn't it? The idea of spending a ton of your time, your energy, and your treasure on a dream with the very real thought in the back of your mind that no one will buy it or like it is daunting. You're even afraid someone might mock you and drag your name through the mud because of it. But let's talk about fear—the big elephant in the room—because I've been exactly where you are.

What part of pursuing your idea scares you the most? What seems to be the most overwhelming aspect? Is it the time it will take? Is it the financial commitment? Fear of the unknown? Fear of failure?

Or is it fear of rejection?

For most people, though intimidating, most fears are easier to handle than the fear of rejection. For some reason having other people judge your idea and, God forbid, not like it is far scarier than anything else you need to deal with. After all, you're awesome right? How can everyone not see that? Surely, they must know about all your amazing qualities. It's impossible to think that some people out there would have the audacity to not like you!

And yet, let me ask you this: Do YOU like everyone? Answer: no. Some people are just downright unlikeable. (Again, not you, of course. I'm speaking of all those *other* people.) But somehow, many of those unlikeable people have succeeded incredibly and have made an impact on the world.

Here's the deal: If you live on planet earth and have been here for any length of time, chances are you've run across somebody who is not exactly your biggest fan. No matter how hard you've tried, you simply could not make them like you. Yet you've still managed to live life and move forward. Why? Because that's what you must do. You need to keep moving, and since you're already moving, why not move in the direction of completing your idea? You might as well. What do you have to lose? Answer: nothing. You have everything to gain.

To put it bluntly, you will never become less intelligent or experienced by trying something.

As a writer and an artist myself, I'm constantly dealing with things I have to show to people. Whether it's a script or a drawing or whatever, I have to take a blank page and fill it with words and/or pictures. I then must show that material to either my team to get them inspired and give them a vision, or I have to submit it to a client or studio in order to get paid, and then I do the most dangerous thing of all: I post it online or license it to a streaming service.

In every single case, there's potential for real rejection or a real sense of insecurity and doubt. Am I the best artist out there? Certainly not! Am I the best writer? No way! You can probably tell that much by reading this book up to this point, but to become a professional in my chosen profession (the animation business), I had to get over the fear of people judging my work negatively and begin to imagine all the people out there who would judge my work positively. After all, I just KNOW there are people out there who are going to respond positively. I only have to think of THEM and not the negative ones. Plus, we have the greatest example of all: Jesus Christ.

Jesus even admitted that He knew everyone wasn't going to like Him. Where did He say this?

*"If the world hates you, you know that it hated Me before it hated you" (John 15:18).*

Jesus was fully aware of the hatred surrounding Him, but He went forward with God's plan anyway. And if Jesus is Lord of your life, and if He lives inside you, then you need to go forward with the plan God has given you as well.

You're probably thinking, *How could anyone hate Jesus? After all, didn't He come to seek and save the lost and help the world? Didn't He feed people and heal them?* Yes. All that is true. And despite all His good deeds, Jesus represented a threat to those who persecuted Him. To them, He represented a change in the way they had always done things. He forced people to look inward and realize that were TOO focused on themselves. Basically, He was a truth-teller. And as much as people say they want to hear the truth, many times they don't. It's just this simple: Sometimes, the one with the ideas (even though the ideas are God-given) is hated because they had the courage to follow their ideas. All of this takes COURAGE.

*Confidence* is knowing you can do something and then doing it. *Courage* is not knowing you can do it but going ahead and trying anyway.

Courage and confidence are two words you need to get used to hearing in your daily life.

## List Five of the Most Courageous People You Can Think Of:

*They can be friends, relatives, famous leaders, innovators, or entrepreneurs who have affected the world in some great and memorable way.*

1.

2.

3.

4.

5.

Now look at the list and see what all these people have in common. If you're honest, you'll see that each one of them faced seemingly overwhelming odds at the outset yet continued forward with their vision.

Many people in the Bible experienced yet realized that, to fulfill the God-given calling on their lives, they had to rule over the fear and not let the fear rule over them. Here is a list of those who experienced fear:

1. Moses

2. Daniel

3. Joseph

4. Esther

5. Gideon

6. Jonah

7. Peter

8. Jesus

Wait. Jesus? Jesus had fear?

Yes, indeed. It says in Luke 22:44:

*And being in agony, He prayed more earnestly. Then His sweat became like great drops of blood falling down to the ground.*

Now this kind of fear is probably much greater than any type of fear that you or I have ever experienced. He was actually in so much agony He sweat blood. Jesus is the Son of Man, which means He experienced everything we ever experienced "but was in all points tempted as we are, yet without sin" (Hebrews 4:15).

But even though Jesus was experiencing this agony, He still went through with His assignment. With Jesus living inside you, you can step into your assignment as all those biblical figures mentioned above did. It's your turn now.

# What Quenches the Creative Fire?

Um … everything? Seriously, if you live on planet earth and have been here for more than a day, you have realized that it seems like nearly everything is designed to get in your way rather than help you along. Don't forget that we face an enemy that wants to stop us at every turn. Why? Because every time a child of God wins, the devil takes a loss, and your job is to make sure that you cause him to lose a lot on a daily basis! But if you aren't strong and equipped, it will be MUCH harder to resist him. This is why it says in Ephesians 6:11 to

*Put on the whole armor of God, that you may be able to stand against the wiles [wicked schemes] of the devil.*

And James 4:7 says to

*Resist the devil and he will flee from you.*

This latter verse is exceptionally powerful because it first tells us to RESIST the devil. This requires an action on our part. The action is to resist. This is a term that means *to stand against.* We stand against the devil as he tries to bring his lies and deceit into our daily lives. When he tells us we can't, we say, "We can!" When he tells us we shouldn't, we tell him, "We should!" When he tells us, "It's no use," we tell him, "You're wrong! It is useful." We must absolutely resist all words, deeds, and actions that come against us to try and quench the creative fire within us.

The LAST THING ON EARTH the devil wants is for you to be able to use your creativity and succeed. Why? Because GOD is creative, and whenever we show off our creativity, the devil is reminded that we are God's children and not his. The devil cannot create ANYTHING, and he cannot stand anyone who can. He will do anything he can do to stop you from being creative because you achieving your desired goal means that he's lost more market share in the human world. How great is it to know that your achievements not only give you an opportunity to advance into enemy territory, but also to put the enemy on his toes and cause him to freak out!

The creative fire is a fire that is controlled completely and totally by YOU. It will burn as brightly as you desire. It simply depends on what type of fuel you use and how often you feed it. If you fuel it with nothing—meaning you never work on your dream and hope that it will fuel itself—you will quickly realize that you will produce nothing. You'll become like millions of others who WANTED to do something—something they've always wanted to do—but produced nothing simply because no effort was put into it. But if you are constantly fueling your fire, then it's simply a matter of time until you see the results.

The fire of desire is a strong thing. It's powerful. And it can be used to make great headway, provided you have the courage and strength to use it.

We fuel this fire in many different ways: observing others, taking classes, testing out different variations, practicing, listening to podcasts about the subject. You get the idea. Desire is a strong thing, but to keep yourself "fired up," you're going to have to make an effort to keep yourself interested in your dream.

Today is the day! Rekindle that fire and re-ignite the desire. It's waiting for you. The Bible says that we reap what we sow (see Galatians 6:7). If all you sow are excuses, then that's all you're going to get in return.

I know this is probably not one of the topics you expected to find in this book, but we must get it out in the open. One of the biggest obstacles we face as creative people is fear. The fear and insecurity of letting others judge our work.

But why do we fear this? Doesn't it say in 2 Timothy 1:7 that God did not give us a spirit of fear? If we're Christians, and we know from Isaiah 54:17 that no weapon formed against us will prosper, then why does the fear sometimes feel so overwhelming? Why is it that, when we finish something we've worked hard on, we are suddenly nervous and insecure when it comes to showing it to people?

It shouldn't be this way! As a Christian creative myself, I speak from experience. There have been many moments in my life as a creator, producer, artist, and writer where I worked very hard on a project and then the time came to show it to people. I was so excited to have completed the accomplishment! But then the strangest thing would happen: I would suddenly feel my pulse quicken, my mouth go dry, my body get hot, and my mind start to go in a million different directions. This is not the ideal way to think. But why would this happen? What happened to the excitement I felt when I first completed the project?

*The fear of man brings a snare (Proverbs 29:25).*

It's the fear of man. That's what I was experiencing. And that's what we creatives need to overcome. If we have the fear of what people think of us or how they will judge our work, then we'll never get anything done or take our work any further than our sketchpad or computer desktop. And why do we fear the judgment of people anyway? Is there a logic to it? No. There isn't.

We feel the fear of being judged because we want everyone to like us. C'mon, you know it's true. Being liked is so much easier than not being liked. When you're liked, life moves along much better, doesn't it? You get more compliments, you get more smiles, and you may even get a free drink at the local coffee shop. That's a fun life, right?

But not everyone is liked all the time, are they? You know the answer to that is no. There's not one person on earth who has ever lived who was liked and admired 24/7 by everyone, and yet a ton of people throughout the centuries have still been able to succeed and achieve their heart's dreams and desires.

So, what's the difference between you and them? Why were those creative people able to achieve but for some reason you find yourself full of doubt and insecurity?

Simple: They overcame the fear.

I'll repeat that: They overcame the fear. The fear was there, but they somehow managed to make the fear so insignificant that it was no longer an obstacle. It no longer mattered. All that mattered was moving forward.

This is the mindset that YOU need to have. But how do you get there?

Keep reading.

I hear this from people all the time: "Well, a little fear is a healthy thing." That is 100 percent incorrect. Any amount of fear is a bad thing. It's not healthy and never will be. Fear exists, yes, but it is an emotion that we can have complete control over as long as we focus on renewing our minds.

*And do not be conformed to this world, but be transformed by the renewing of your mind, that you may prove what is that good and acceptable and perfect will of God (Romans 12:2).*

As creative Christians, we MUST renew our minds and retrain them in thinking that our ideas are awesome, our ideas matter, and our ideas can and WILL be successful! Think of it this way: We've already spent so much time living in the negative mindset—or the NEGATIVE ZONE—that, sometimes, we don't even realize we are living there because we have been there so long. We don't have an idea there's even an alternative way to live!

Whether we've had bad experiences, had bad words spoken to us, or simply did not believe in ourselves, somehow, we ended up in the negative zone. It's now time to move into a new zone called CONFIDENCE. Life is much better in the confidence zone, trust me. It took me some time to get there myself, but once I was inside the confidence zone, I had zero desire to leave.

It takes work and a renewed and changed mindset to become confident. And it will ONLY happen if you apply yourself to this idea. You must think and say to yourself daily: "I am a winner. I am confident. I deserve to be successful." This is a godly principle from Scripture:

*Death and life are in the power of the tongue, and those who love it will eat its fruit (Proverbs 18:21)*

We have the power of death and life in our tongue. "In our tongue" refers to what we speak or say. The words we speak over ourselves are incredibly important. You don't think words have power? How did God create the world?

*Then God said, "Let there be light"; and there was light (Genesis 1:3).*

Your words always matter. Speaking life over yourself is a must. You must always remember to not say negative words or phrases over your work or yourself as you step into what God has given you to do. Don't fall into the habit of saying things like: "Oh, I'll never succeed," or "I'm just not good at this," or "This will NEVER work!" If you say such things, what do you think will happen?

You will have what you say. Exactly.

Try saying more things like this over yourself: "I'm a winner! I can do this! This WILL be successful!"

Remember when I said not to say, "A little fear is a healthy thing"? We need to replace the word *fear* with *wisdom.* "A little WISDOM is a healthy thing," is what we should be saying. Gaining as much

WISDOM as possible is what we need to focus on, not the fear. The older we get, the wiser we are. There's just no arguing that point. God tells us in His Word that wisdom is to be more valued than any treasure:

*Happy is the man who finds wisdom, and the man who gains understanding; for her proceeds are better than the profits of silver, and her gain than fine gold. She is more precious than rubies, and all the things you may desire cannot compare with her (Proverbs 3:13–17).*

Searching for wisdom as you follow your dream should be first on your list of priorities. Let's face it, we all need instruction and understanding no matter what we're trying to achieve, right? Going into our chosen field with no knowledge can not only be foolish, but it can also be dangerous. It may end up costing us not only financially, but physically. God isn't telling us to shy away from finances— they can be a major blessing when in the right hands— but He is telling us to not elevate finances higher than wisdom. Wisdom will take us farther and into greater places than finances alone ever could. Now, if you couple your wisdom with finances, that's a recipe for success every time.

I know it's not easy to conquer fear. But it has to – it must – be dealt with. If you don't deal with it you will be subject to it and that is not going to help you. I strongly encourage you to face it.

Once you face it, then it will cease to have power over you.

## List Some Things You Used to Fear:

# Is This the Right Time?

"Butch, you just don't understand my situation, I am simply not in the right place to begin my idea."

Well, few people are ever in the right place to begin pursuing their ideas, yet the successful individuals begin anyway despite the fear or concern about timing. Our job as Christians is to overcome the fear and keep moving.

That's an important word: OVERCOME.

In *Mark 11:24, Jesus tells us to speak to the mountain, and it will be removed and cast into the sea.* It doesn't say that Jesus will speak to the mountain for us. It says that WE are to speak to the mountain— or obstacle—ourselves. Jesus wants US to make the decisions and get empowered by the success they produce. And one major thing we can overcome is the excuse we make when it comes to beginning our journey to the goal. See if any of following sound familiar:

1. "This isn't the right time."

2. "I have too many other things going on."

3. "I don't have the energy."

4. "I'll get to it next week."

5. "No one is going to like this anyway."

6. "I'll never be able to pull this off."

7. "I don't have enough money to get started."

Excuses are easy to make but very difficult to throw away. They can change the course of your life if you keep making them. But if you stop making them, you can take your life in directions you never thought possible. Sure, there will be difficulties along the way, but it's up to you to decide whether you're ready to grow up and move on.

It's like the story in John 5.

## The Man at the Pool of Bethesda

This man—a man who had a sickness—lay at the pool of Bethesda, which was thought to have healing powers. Many people were so sure that this pool of water had healing power that, whenever the water was stirred, they would fight tooth and nail to be the first one in so they could receive their healing. This man lay at that pool for 38 years and, for some reason, could not get into the water first. When he was asked a very simple question by Jesus: "Do you want to be healed?" Or, in other words, "Do you want to make a new life for yourself?" The man had several responses he could have given. "Yes" would have been a good one, but the man did not say that. Instead, he told the Lord that there was no one to put him in the water (see John 5:7).

The man started blaming others for his problem! Instead of saying, "Yes, Lord, I want to be healed," he started making excuses.

Let's look at why he would do something like that.

I mean, after all, he had been lying there for 38 years, right? I don't know about you, but 38 years seems like a VERY long time to me. You'd think after 38 years the man would be more than eager to be healed, wouldn't you?

But sometimes people SAY they want something when they really don't mean it.

After all, this man had lain at that pool for 38 years—13,870 days— and had NEVER gotten into the pool first. How does that happen? Put yourself in that position. If you truly wanted to be healed, then wouldn't you do everything possible to get into that pool? What was stopping him?

Simple, he became IDENTIFIED with being sick. It became WHO HE WAS, and he simply COULD NOT SEE HIMSELF HEALED.

Here's a question for you: CAN YOU EVEN SEE YOURSELF BECOMING A SUCCESS? CAN YOU GET INTO THE POOL OF SUCCESS EVEN THOUGH EVERYONE ELSE IS FIGHTING TO GET IN, TOO?

The reason the man—the reason ANY OF US—become identified with our circumstances is because we simply cannot see ourselves doing anything else, and this only gets worse as we get older. The old habits and beliefs get harder to break. But it is the TRUE VISIONARY—the one with THE MIND OF CHRIST—who can overcome old habits and beliefs and begin to see themselves as a conqueror, as a champion, as a leader, and as a successful creative Christian.

The man at the pool had two choices to make when Jesus told him to take up his bed and walk (see John 5:8):

1. He could stay in his situation. He could stay by the pool with all the other sick people and keep making excuses and never get his desire. He could keep doing the same old thing he'd been doing for so long, or—

2. He could get up. But getting up required something enormous of him: the desire to live life in a different way. Getting up meant many things. He would have to now live life as a healthy, able-bodied person, which he had not done for 38 years. He would now have to begin life again as a working person who could now care for himself. He would most likely have to get a job and become responsible. This required a lot of bravery. Do you think the world—the marketplace—had changed in the 38 years he lay by the pool? Indeed, it had. It took a lot of guts on his part to face up to that.

I point all this out because I want you to consider your choices as you move forward:

1. You can stay in the same place you've been for the last 38 years (or whatever length of time it's been), or you can take up your bed—your old way of thinking—and move on.

2. When Jesus asks you the question, "Are you ready to make a new life for yourself?" you can begin to make excuses, or you can say, "Yes, Lord," even though you don't exactly know what's ahead of you.

3. You can back down and recoil because of the looks and attitudes all your friends and family make or have toward you as you tried to make the choice to move up to a new level, or you can move past that and do what Jesus told you to do.

The choice is up to you. Time to take up your bed and walk. You've lain in the same place long enough.

# Great Drops of Blood

Newsflash: This is hard work. There are no two ways about it. Think about what Jesus went through in the Garden of Gethsemane just before He was crucified:

*And being in agony, He prayed more earnestly. Then His sweat became like great drops of blood falling down to the ground (Luke 22:44).*

He was struggling massively with the spiritual and physical challenges that were before Him. Now, I'm not saying that pursuing your goal is ANYTHING even close to what Jesus went through, but to some of us it can certainly FEEL like we are going through the same thing. For some folks, even making that first phone call can seem like a monumental task. (The word *mental* is even in the word *monumental.* Must be something "mental" about it, huh?) Building anything is hard. It's going to take a lot out of you, but it DOESN'T HAVE TO IF YOU DON'T ALLOW IT TO!

As creative people, we face challenges and obstacles every day. *What do I draw today? What do I write? What do I compose, sculpt, build, erase, increase, paint, or sell?* The list is endless, and it can be daunting for anyone, but thank goodness we have a Savior who has our best interests at heart. The Bible tells us that we should "be anxious for NOTHING" (Philippians 4:6).

"Don't be anxious for anything" is another way to say it so that must mean it's an option for us, right? I mean, if we have the option to "not be anxious," then we must also, conversely, have the option TO be anxious should we so choose to be.

Jesus said, "Come to me all of you who are burdened and heavy laden and I will give you rest...." That last word is important: rest. Jesus didn't say "I'll give you an extra burden." We don't go to Jesus for a heavier load. We go to Him so He will take the load. That is what He wants. As creative people, we sometimes can get bogged down with all the tasks and minutiae that comes with accomplishing our goal. Jesus wants us to cast "all [our] care on Him, for He cares for [us]" (1 Peter 5:7). It is incredibly reassuring to know that as a creative—especially a Christian one—we have an Advocate who not only wants us to succeed, but who wants us to do it without sweating "great drops of blood." We'll sweat, that's true, but the anguish that He went through never even needs to come near us if we choose not to have it.

We need to LOVE what we do. I always say that, if you love what you do, you'll never work a day in your life. Will you work hard? Yes. Will you have to become completely drained? No. The choice is yours. Be anxious for NOTHING!

Name Some Things You Could Potentially Be Anxious About:

# Desire Drives the Day

*Delight yourself in the Lord, and He will give you the desires of your heart (Psalm 37:4).*

What is it you love to do the most? Or what do you do every day of your own volition that no one has to ask you to do? Think about that for a minute. Everyone knows that, when we get some time on our hands, we do that certain thing that we love the most.

Now, let me share something insightful with you: That's what you should be doing for a living—the thing that you love to do the most.

*Gasp!* "But, Butch, you mean I can build Lego sculptures for a living?"

Yes! There are some serious Lego sculptors out there who have artistic portfolios containing all their amazing work! They have high-end gallery showcases of their sculptures, and some even have highly successful YouTube channels, too!

"You mean I can knit quilts for a living?"

Absolutely! There are some majorly successful folks out there who do exactly that and more! They made their hobby into an industry from which they get to make a living, AND they get to do what they love every day.

If you love it, make a living out of it!

When you decide what it truly is that wakes you up in the morning and what drives you, then you will eliminate 95 percent of all the obstacles that stand in your way. When you have a clear path, a clear focus, a clear goal, and you know exactly what it is, then all your life decisions will be based on that particular goal.

Take me for example. I knew very early on in life—at around 10 years of age—that I wanted to draw cartoons for a living. Didn't matter where or when or for how much money, the main thing was that I wanted to draw and create all the time, and so I needed to find the place or places where I could do that. I had to take other odd jobs along the way as I searched for the various outlets that allowed me to draw more and more, but the desire to draw and create led me to where I am today. I needed to travel to it, live near it, be immersed in it, hang out with people who did it and, ultimately, become employed by businesses and studios that produced it. In short, my desire drove my day. It can drive yours, too.

But don't expect someone else to drive it for you.

## Name Some Things You Love to Do and Would Love to Make a Living Doing:

# The Purpose of Your Creativity

*So God created man in His own image; in the image of God He created him; male and female He created them (Genesis 1:27).*

There is so much creativity going on! We live in a world where we see things created every single day. People create cars, buildings, cell phones, computers, recipes, clothing, books, movies, poems, sandwiches, paintings, cartoons, and lots and lots of problems! (The good news is they can create solutions, too!)

My point is: CREATIVITY IS ALL AROUND YOU ALL THE TIME!

Think about it: YOU were created! You didn't just randomly appear like a rabbit in a magic trick. That's what society wants us to think sometimes. People want you to think that you are here completely randomly, and your life and existence have no meaning other than waking up, going to work, paying bills, and then growing old. That is incorrect! Your existence here is no accident. You were MEANT to be here.

*Even before he made the world, God loved us and chose us in Christ... (Ephesians 1:4 NLT).*

We are supposed to make the most of our time here. God wants us to use every gift He's ever given us, and we have been given more than one. Why have them go to waste? We don't need to use them all at once, but we need to at least begin to explore them one at a time.

Let's look at a story in the Bible where we see how important our gifts and talents are to God.

## The Parable of the Talents (Matthew 25:14–20)

In the parable of the talents, the master rewarded the two stewards who multiplied his money. They were told, "Well done, good and faithful servant" (Matthew 25:21, 23). In fact, the master gave them even more. But the one who did nothing with his gift—the one who was afraid and buried it—the master not only got angry with, but he called him a "wicked and lazy" servant (Matthew 25:26)! He even cast him into outer darkness! Yikes! (Yes. I said, "Yikes." I'm a cartoon lover. What can I say?)

Jesus gave us this parable to keep us aware of the fact that our talents, our gifts, our CREATIVITY, and His investment in us are very important to Him. He doesn't want us taking what He has given us and burying it like the lazy servant. He wants all of us to use that creativity to create. He wants us to let our light shine and be seen!

*"No one lights a lamp and then puts it under a basket" (Matthew 5:15 NLT).*

You see, you were created with a PURPOSE!

"What? Really? I have a purpose?" you may ask.

That's right. It took two people coming together (your mom and dad, not to mention the dozens of ancestors that came before them) to get you here, but here you are. GOD WORKED THROUGH ALL THOSE PEOPLE to put you here. For this time. And here you are. Say that to yourself on a daily basis: "I was put here for this time."

*"Yet who knows whether you have come to the kingdom for such a time as this?" (Esther 4:14).*

And now you have a lot of decisions to make.

Oh wait? Don't like making decisions? Okay. That's fine. Then I guarantee decisions will be made for you. If you can't decide where to live, what to do, what to wear, or what to believe, then trust me, those decisions will be made for you. It's just a fact of life.

Don't believe me? Think of a prison. Criminals of all kinds have somehow—because of BAD decisions—ended up behind bars, and now nearly all their freedoms and decision making have been taken away from them. They are told where to walk, when to eat, and when to sleep. Prison life is a life that can be lived, but it is not the ideal life. It is not the life of freedom that God has in store for you. We serve a God—a Savior—Jesus Christ. And He came to earth and gave His life for you so that you would no longer be enslaved. So that you could be free. Free to live a life that allows you to explore all that God has to offer. And He offered you the creative gifts He has given you. And there is no real way to explore creative gifts in a prison. You need to be free—unbound—so that your creativity can soar! Let it flow!

But the one thing that stops creativity every time is something we use (or misuse) every day: our minds.

## Name Some Decisions You Hate to Make:

# Has Your Mind Imprisoned You?

Thoughts. They're free and they never stop. They flow, and they flow, and without a control system in place—like a faucet or traffic light—they'll just keep right on flowing. Sometimes, they'll flow so much that you feel overwhelmed, out-of-control. We can feel overwhelmed by negative thoughts, but sometimes positive thoughts can even be a challenge. Have you ever had a time where there are so many great things going on that you can't get ahold of yourself? Too much of a good thing can sometimes be "too much" if you don't know how to properly steward it.

What the creative Christian needs is a way to control their thoughts so they produce positive results only. The Lord said in Genesis 1:28, "Be fruitful and multiply." Multiplication is what the Lord is all about! He's 100 percent about growth and improvement. BUT, He only wants multiplication of GOOD things, not bad. After all, why would the Almighty, the all-powerful God of the Universe, go to all the trouble of bringing us here only to have us DECREASE instead of INCREASE. He wants us to grow in all good things in order that we may glorify Him. And the only way we can increase and grow is if our minds are free. Worry, concern, and anxiety are all growth-blockers, and we must do everything we can to get rid of those thoughts and replace them with thoughts of positivity, joy, and peace.

*Finally, brethren, whatever things are true, whatever*

*things are noble, whatever things are just, whatever things are pure,*

*whatever things are lovely, whatever things are of good report, if there is any virtue and if there is anything praiseworthy—meditate on these things (Philippians 4:8).*

Why does the Lord want us thinking about just good things? Pure things? Lovely things? Things of good report? Virtuous things? Praiseworthy things? Because these things lead to good thoughts and good thoughts lead to joy and joy leads to creativity. We simply MUST work toward opening our minds to the idea that life can have many joyous things about it if we know where to look. The problem is that sometimes the world of man speaks louder than the Word of God. It is completely up to US to silence the negativity and turn up the volume on the positivity.

Find the freedom in God's Word. Make Bible reading and spending quality time with the Lord a part of your daily routine. When you meditate (think about) the things of God instead of the things of the world, you'll begin to notice dramatic change in your creative output.

Do not be a prisoner of your own thoughts. As a creative person, I'll bet you've experienced at least one of—if not all—of the following thoughts:

1. *I'm not good enough.*

2. *I'm not smart enough.*

3. *Nobody wants what I am offering.*

4. *I'm scared to start.*

5. *People will laugh at me.*

6. *I'll fail and be embarrassed.*

I could keep going, but you get the idea. Every single one of us have had thoughts like these. When I was doing animated TV shows in Hollywood, I would have these thoughts several times EVERY SINGLE MINUTE! The entertainment business is a definite pressure cooker, and you are constantly being scrutinized as to how well your project is going, how many people are watching, and most importantly, how much money it is making. In my profession, I was in charge of several staffs at once, each consisting of dozens of people. If my projects failed and had to get cancelled, that meant people would lose their jobs, and that was something I would think about every day. Had I not had the Word of God in my life, I would have instantly turned to the world's (society's) way of thinking and gone down a dark road of negativity and fear. I would have allowed the pressure to get at me, and it would have affected everything, particularly my health and my family.

I wasn't about to let that happen, so I turned to Jesus, and He pointed me to scripture after scripture that told me how victorious I was and could be:

*We are more than conquerors through Him who loved us (Romans 8:37).*

Once I got hold of those truths, I was able to put the pressure aside and focus on the joy of the job instead of all the seemingly endless challenges. And, trust me, there are TONS of challenges when you are dealing with producing a television show. Things were NOT always rosy, believe me, but it was in those tough times I was able to practice freeing my mind from the negative and focus on the positive.

There will be a great many challenges when it comes to realizing your dream, and you need to know that conquerors do one thing well: They CONQUER! That means they win! You are a WINNER, and like every other winner in every other thing ever in life, you will have to overcome obstacles to succeed. But getting over obstacles makes you stronger not weaker.

Your mind is your greatest weapon when it comes to your creativity. This is why the enemy wants it full of distractions that block any source of creative energy. Whatever is in your mind will have one of two effects: positive or negative. When things are positive, awesome growth can happen. When things are negative, however, we take a step backward, but we don't want that.

Free your mind. This is a must. Only with a clear focus will you be able to move down the field. Ask Jesus to help you.

### List Some Things You Can Let Go of to Focus on Your Goal:

1.

2.

3.

4.

# Immerse Yourself

One way to stay motivated is to immerse yourself in an atmosphere of like-minded individuals who love what you love and want to do the same thing as you. If you want to be a better baseball player, you should hang out with baseball players. If you want to be a better violin player, then hang out with violin players. It's the immersion in the atmosphere that will help you stay motivated. You'll be constantly talking about your favorite subject, working on different techniques, and challenging each other with different ideas about the topic.

When I was a young artist wanting to work in the professional animation industry, who do you think I hung out with the most? That's right, professional bowlers! I'm kidding! No, I hung out 24/7 with other animation students and professionals. I couldn't get enough of what I loved because we constantly talked about animation, took art classes, and attended animation lectures and watched animated movies. It was what I loved, and I was determined to learn as much about it as I could.

If you love a certain topic or discipline and want to make it your profession, then it is 100 percent your responsibility to be around it as much as you possibly can. If for some reason you find it difficult to create that type of atmosphere around you at the current time, then create as much of a creative atmosphere as you can. Do what's necessary to wake up your spirit and keep that spiritual fire burning within. I'm here to tell you firsthand that God wants this kind of atmosphere around you. He wants you creating things 24/7. He is excited for you! Even more excited than you are for yourself! But He wants that spirit inside you firing brighter than ever. If your spirit is NOT burning brightly, then something is stopping it from doing so.

Let's figure it out.

## WHY?

It's only a three-letter word, but it carries a lot of power.

There's a reason for everything, and you need to know yours. What's the "why" behind your "what"? You bought this book to gain some information that would help you in reaching your intended goal, so you'd better be SUPER clear on why you're doing it. Yes, you can absolutely start down the road without the clearest plan (hey, it happens in politics every day), BUT isn't it going to be much better when you start off with a firm foundation? With a clear reason for all the time and effort you're about to put in? Take it from someone who has pursued MANY goals: It is always better to have purpose behind the plan.

There will be many days and nights where you feel that you're the only one on earth who cares about what it is you're doing, and you know what? You're right! If you are simply following your pursuit for the applause, then you may as well stop now. The applause won't come for a while, and even when it does, it won't come very often. You need to do your thing because you feel it needs to be done. Period.

## Why Are You Pursuing This Goal of Yours?

*Be specific! This is not a time to be vague. Get clear on the reasons why.*

1.

2.

3.

4.

# Prepare for the Opportunity

The parable of the wise and foolish virgins in Matthew 25:1–13 is extremely eye-opening in many ways. It tells the story of two sets of virgins who were waiting for the bridegroom to come—the wise ones and the foolish ones. Basically, the wise ones had oil in their lamps and were prepared for the bridegroom to come and get them. The foolish ones were not prepared and had no oil even though they had had time to prepare for the bridegroom's coming just as the wise ones did. The foolish ones even asked the wise ones if they could borrow some of their oil, and the wise ones said that they could not loan the foolish any oil at all because, if they did, then none of them would have had enough (see Matthew 25:8). So, the foolish had to leave to get oil while the wise were prepared and got to go with the bridegroom when the opportunity came.

Now, we know that this parable is talking about saved people (the wise) and unsaved people (the foolish) being prepared for the second coming of Jesus (the bridegroom). But let's look at it in a different way which isn't detracting from the original meaning but can be applied to each and every Christian creative as we pursue our goals.

There are opportunities that present themselves to every creative person. Be they a friend who asks you to draw something for their son's birthday, the local school that asks you to bake a batch of your awesome cookies for the bake sale, or the relative that just loves your table centerpieces and suggests that you decorate for the big graduation party. Whatever the opportunity is, we need to always be prepared because we never know where that opportunity may lead.

If we look at the bridegroom as an OPPORTUNITY and the wise and foolish virgins as THE PREPARED and THE UNPREPARED, respectively, perhaps we can begin to more clearly see how we can apply the teaching of this parable to our own goals.

Here is a personal example. When I was first starting out in the Hollywood animation business, I was working at Hanna-Barbera Studios. (You may know them as the studio that created *The Flintstones, Scooby Doo,* and many other cartoons.) There was never an opportunity to create your own show while you were employed there. If you were hired as an artist (like me) to work on a project, you would do your job 9 to 5 and go home. You were really never asked your opinion on much, and the only people who could create a show or generate any new ideas were the execs in charge. That was pretty much the way it was. Getting a chance to pitch an idea for a new show or movie was a very rare and valuable opportunity, and it didn't come around very often, if at all. The mindset of most people in the industry those day was: *I just want a job, and I'm good. Hopefully someone will hire me.* And that was totally understandable. That was my attitude as well.

I guess you could say, at that time, I was in the category of the foolish or unprepared.

But as I spent more time in the animation world working at Hanna-Barbera, I began to get restless. I was working on some programming that I wasn't very excited about. There really was nothing wrong with it, but it just wasn't the kind of stuff that made me want to get up each morning and go do it. To me it wasn't compelling. And quite honestly, I felt I could make stuff a lot better on my own. Entertainment projects with more comedy and cooler characters. I just needed an opportunity for someone to see my ideas, but as I said, that sort of opportunity simply didn't exist at the time. Would it ever exist? Should I have stopped preparing new ideas of my own?

What would you do?

Well, I'm certainly glad I didn't stop because one day an opportunity came—one that would change my life. And the best part? I was prepared.

I had been at the studio for about a year when Hanna-Barbera was bought by Turner Broadcasting. They planned to create a brand-new cable channel called the Cartoon Network, and Turner Broadcasting was offering all of us at the studio the opportunity to pitch new ideas to them. Brand new ideas made by us, the artists.

Wait. What? WE had the opportunity to pitch NEW IDEAS to them? We regular artists? They wanted to hear us? But I NEVER thought an opportunity like that would happen!

But it finally did.

Fortunately for me, I had been preparing. I had been developing ideas on my own like the wise and prepared virgins, and once there was an opportunity (like the bridegroom's arrival), I was able to pitch my ideas to the studio. The studio even bought a few of them, and I was suddenly on my way from becoming more than just an artist. I was now becoming a PRODUCER. I was increasing my skill set and my experience. The other folks around me who had not been preparing—and had no intention of preparing—let the opportunity pass them by and were never able to take advantage of it again.

I often say that great opportunities are like comets. You know the ones that fly through space? They look really amazing and might be quite dazzling as they pass by, but they don't come around very often. And it might be a very long time until you see another one again.

Seize the opportunity! Be like the wise virgins. Have oil in your lamp. Be ready. The bridegroom —the opportunity—is coming!

## Answer the Following Questions about Preparing for Opportunity:

1. What ideas have you been preparing?

2. What opportunities are you waiting for?

3. Does "preparing" seem like hard work to you or does it seem fun?

4. What sort of "oil" (items) do you need to prepare for the opportunity?

# You Can Do It!

I know that phrase is so overused in our culture—to the point that saying it almost means nothing sometimes. BUT I MEAN IT: YOU. CAN. DO. IT.

Let's break that sentence down, shall we?

1. YOU—This is talking about you. The one reading this. The one whose face you see in the mirror every day. The one you've seen your whole life.

2. CAN—This word means able. You are able to do what you choose to do. But just because we find ourselves able to do something doesn't mean we have to. The decision to DO IT or NOT DO IT is up to us. The most interesting thing about the word *can* is that it has a direct opposite relative in the word *can't*. Let's replace *can* with *can't* and read the sentence again: YOU CAN'T DO THIS. See? That is not a very fun sentence, yet it has just as much validity as the first sentence. So, when we say, "YOU CAN DO THIS," the CAN part is YOUR choice. You can either allow yourself to do it or not. It's all up to you.

3. DO—This is a verb meaning action. It's the ability to do something. If you can think it, you can do it, if you allow yourself to believe that of course.

4. IT—This is the thing. It's the *whatever* you're doing. It's the dream – your dream - that's going to change the world.

Just wanted to be clear on that sentence. You are totally the one who decides whether the goal can be accomplished. People much less talented and with far fewer resources than you have done amazing things in the world, so there should be no excuses. Yes, I know challenges come, I know family situations happen, I know money is tight, and I know you're a Christian person trying to create something awesome in a world that hates Jesus. But guess what? You can do this.

## List Some Big Decisions You've Made Lately and Why You Made Them:

*Keep your answers simple and direct.*

Now that you've been reminded of some big decisions you've made, let's start making some new ones.

Ready? Let's make some plans!

# Section 2: Application or Creation

We're already inspired and fired up! We are ready to rock 'n' roll and get moving. But how do we begin to apply ourselves toward achieving our goal? How do we begin to create the idea?

List some thoughts on how to begin making your idea a reality:

1.

2.

3.

4.

5.

# Having a Plan

Before you start anything, you must have a plan if you're smart, that is. (I'm assuming you are because you bought this amazing book!)

(Insert polite laugh here.)

Planning gives us the opportunity to "count the cost" of what it's going to take to make our goal a reality. Check out this scripture:

*"For which of you, intending to build a tower, does not sit down first and count the cost, whether he has enough to finish it?" (Luke 14:28).*

We must take stock of what it is we're doing and how much time it will take to do it. Now, before the panic sets in, don't worry. I know there is no real way to know EXACTLY how long things will take or EXACTLY how much things will cost, BUT it is better to estimate and have a game plan than to go into the game with no strategy at all. However, the more exact and precise you can be with your planning the better start you'll have.

For example, in writing this book, I gave myself a rough timeline for completion: six months. I figured I could get everything down that I had in my heart in that amount of time. I didn't say, "6 months, 3 weeks, 2 days, and 9 hours." Heck, if I could pull that off, I would be very impressed with myself!

(Insert another polite laugh here.)

But what I was able to do was give myself a deadline, even though it was a rough one. If you give yourself a deadline—and force yourself to stick to it—you'll find that you become a much more intentional person. A person with a deadline is a person who has a goal. And a person with a goal will eventually become a person who meets the goal. Having a goal, a deadline, is part of counting the cost.

You may also have to give a few things up. Things that take time away from you heading to the goal. A lot of us spend too much time "wasting time," and it pushes our dream farther and farther down the road. That's not to say you can't enjoy yourself and do things occasionally that AREN'T related to your goal, but you need to ask yourself this question: "How important is my goal to me?"

Seriously. Think about that: How important is it? Some people will use a camera to take a picture and be done with it. But to some people, taking a picture is EVERYTHING. It's a form of expression that, to them, IS EVERYTHING. When your goal becomes EVERYTHING to you, then you'll be more motivated to accomplish it.

How important is this dream to you? What will you set aside to make room for it?

## List Some Things You Need to Move Aside to Make More Time for Your Goal:

1.

2.

3.

Another question to ask yourself, even if you may not know the answer is: "How much time will this cost me?" Remember: You may not know how much time it will take, but you have to start somewhere, and that's what successful people do: They start.

This step, making a plan, is where a lot of us creative types stall out. It's always great to dream of things and to imagine them being real and enjoying the benefits. Kind of like going to the store and buying a cake that has already been baked. But it's in the baking of the cake that we truly grow and learn.

Making a plan involves a lot of thinking and strategy. It's where we actually begin to put the puzzle together in our heads and start to see how we can truly make our chosen goal a reality.

Make a plan.

Count the cost.

Get started.

## List Some of the Items or Resources You Will Need to Get Started on Your Plan:

*These can be physical things or even the contact information of different people.*

1.

2.

3.

# Resources

Let's face it. You can't start a fire without wood. You can't bake a cake without the ingredients. You can't build a house without nails. You get the idea. Plans are very necessary, but the materials, resources, and connections needed to carry them out are just as important. And as Christian creatives, we need those things to assist us in achieving our goals.

Let's look to the Bible and read a story about resources. It's the parable of the Good Samaritan. Jesus tells the story in Luke 10:30–37:

*Then Jesus answered and said: "A certain man went down from Jerusalem to Jericho, and fell among thieves, who stripped him of his clothing, wounded him, and departed, leaving him half dead. Now by chance a certain priest came down that road. And when he saw him, he passed by on the other side. Likewise a Levite, when he arrived at the place, came and looked, and passed by on the other side. But a certain Samaritan, as he journeyed, came where he was. And when he saw him, he had compassion. So he went to him and bandaged his wounds, pouring on oil and wine; and he set him on his own animal, brought him to an inn, and took care of him. On the next day, when he departed, he took out two denarii, gave them to the innkeeper, and said to him, 'Take care of him; and whatever more you spend, when I come again, I will repay you.' So which of these*

*three do you think was neighbor to him who fell among the thieves?"
And he said, "He who showed mercy on him." Then Jesus said to
him, "Go and do likewise."*

Now, we can use this story to teach a great many truths; however,
for now, I want to focus on one particular aspect: RESOURCES.

What did the Good Samaritan have? He had a good heart, that's
number one (Luke 10:33 says he had compassion), but he had a very
key element that aided him in helping the man who had been
injured by bandits and left half dead on the side of the road.

The Good Samaritan had RESOURCES! Yes, he had the means to
help the man. Having a good heart is a very important thing, and we
should all strive to have one so the Lord can use us. If we have no
resources, however, then our help and ability to aid will be severely
limited. Let's look at what the Samaritan had:

- He had physical and medical aid available: bandages, oil, and
  wine (see Luke 10:36). He had medical help and supply.

- He had his own animal (see Luke 10:34). His animal was
  essentially his vehicle. Animals were the cars or trucks during
  those times, so that Samaritan not only had medical aid
  available, he had a vehicle at the ready, which was valuable
  in getting the injured man to care.

- He had connections and finances. He was well aware of what
  was available by way of lodging in the local area. He was able
  to pay for the wounded man's room, providing him with a
  safe place to stay (see Luke 10:34). He was able to give
  money to the inn keeper to take care of and tend to any

needs the injured man had. He had finances to repay for any additional care or needs (see Luke 10:35).

- So, the Samaritan not only had enough to pay for the man's room for one night, the Samaritan had enough money to pay for a lengthy stay for the man! One more thing: The Good Samaritan had to leave the man at the inn for a while because the Samaritan had one more resource—business to do. Yes. The Samaritan had a purpose. He had things to do, business to attend to. This is something a lot of us need to realize: We need to have a focus. A purpose. Business to take care of.

- And to take it even further, the Samaritan had yet another resource: flexibility. He obviously had no idea he would encounter the wounded man on the side of the road, yet he altered his schedule, took time out of his life, to attend to the man and see to it that he was cared for before he got back to his own schedule.

If the Samaritan had no resources—if he had been a beggar and had nothing of his own, no possessions, vehicle, connections, finances, or flexibility—he would never had been able to even help himself much less anyone else.

Resources are an extremely important thing that all creative Christians need to have. You may not have all the resources you need right now, but keep moving with the ones you DO have. Better to move and get what you need along the way than to be frozen in place and never acquire anything.

List the Resources the Good Samaritan Had:

1.

2.

3.

4.

## List Some of the Resources You Currently Have:

1.

2.

3.

4.

## List Some of the Resources You Need:

1.

2.

3.

4.

After you have listed the resources that you need, pray for God to provide them for you. It says in Philippians 4:19, "And my God shall supply all your need according to His riches in glory by Christ Jesus."

Praying for God to supply us with resources is, in itself, a fantastic resource we have as Christian creatives!

# The Team

This is a big one. Don't freak out, and don't close the book and run away just yet. We're only talking here. Right now, all I want you to do is dream. Dream about the perfect set of people you can put around you to make this thing that is within you happen.

Yes. I said, "People you can put around you." See, NOTHING hugely successful can happen without a team. Nothing. Even when you watch a world class tennis player or golfer (a sport where the player is on their own), there is a massive team that you don't see behind them. Trainers, coaches, lawyers, advertising people, family that supported them before they were famous. It is a massive support system of people that gets us where we want to be. But the genius of the successful people is that an illusion is created that makes it seem like they did it all alone. This could also apply to famous actors, politicians, musicians, or other such people. A team of supportive people is helping them along the way.

You're going to need a team, too. Even Jesus had a team! The 12 disciples! Yes, He's Jesus, and He could have done everything on His own (since He is the Creator of the Universe), but He wanted a team around Him for several reasons:

1.  Fellowship—Jesus loved to be around people. He loved family. He created us to fellowship with one another, and it's through His example that we can learn how to fellowship, too.

2.  Training—Jesus was training His followers on how to be like Him, how to run His ministry, and how to walk in the

vision He was putting before them. Without spending time with Jesus, they never would have known what He was thinking or how He wanted to do things.

3. Legacy—Jesus knew He had to train people to continue His vision after He went to Heaven. We need to plan for the same thing! Think about it: Do you want everything you've worked for to simply end after you've left to be with Jesus? When we do something successful, and it starts to change our lives and our family's lives for the better, then we definitely want to make sure we leave it in the hands of people who can continue the legacy long after we are gone.

Now, remember, we are just talking here. No need to panic. But I wanted to make sure you know that having a team is very important. It forces you to become a leader. Why? Because the team will need to know what their mission is. And, hey, if you created the mission, then who better than you to relay it to others?

"But, Butch," you might be saying, "I'm a bit of an introvert and not good with teams. I need to be alone to do my best work."

I've heard this before and heard it countless times, and I'm not negating it, but I AM telling you that you will get FAR LESS done and will proceed FAR MORE SLOWLY if you do things alone.

Let me ask you something. When did the serpent approach Eve? Was she with Adam at the time, or was she alone? It's not really clear but the bottom line is: her team failed her.

The enemy went to Eve when she was the most vulnerable to suggestion and – whether he was there with her or not - Adam was no help. In fact, he went along with the deception.

The enemy does his best work on us when we are alone. And even though we may have people around us, if they are not quality people we may as well be alone. And many of us have been fooled into thinking we don't need anyone else. The devil has done his best to isolate us from each other for so long that, sometimes, we don't even realize it's happening.

One thing the devil hates more than anything is family. Why? Because a family means strength. And if you're strong, then he can't win. This is why a team is important. People have different strengths and different attitudes. Trust me, as a professional animation writer, creator, executive producer, and entrepreneur, I found out very quickly just how valuable a team – a quality team - can be.

Newsflash: Your entire team will not appear overnight. I think we all know that. It takes time to surround yourself with people you can fully trust. This may take a while, but you HAVE to start somewhere. This is what creative entrepreneurs do: They start. Unfortunately, you will have to cut some people loose along the way, and some people may downright betray you (Judas, anyone?). Yet you can also meet amazing people you'll begin to draw closer into your inner circle. (Peter, James, and John ring a bell?) This is all part of the process as you proceed down the road to your inevitable goal.

A team is necessary, and it's in your growth as a Christian creative that you'll see you can step outside yourself and your insecurities to become a leader of others who will begin to help you build the vision that God has placed in your heart.

Name Some People Who would Make Good Team Members and Why:

1.

2.

3.

4.

# Wise as a Serpent, Harmless as a Dove

Serpents are subtle. They don't make a lot of noise as they move in on their intended target. They must be subtle because they have very little with which to defend themselves. Yes, some carry poison, but if they miss their target, they have nothing else with which to attack and will have to wait for another opportunity which may not come.

On the other hand, doves are very tranquil birds. When people think of scary and violent things, they never think of a dove. Quite the opposite. It was a dove that Noah sent from the ark when the rain finally stopped and they began their search for dry ground. The dove returned with an olive branch in its mouth, indicating that there was land nearby (see Genesis 8:10–11). This is why both the dove AND the olive branch are used to depict peace and hope. So why am I pointing out the differences between a serpent and a dove? Because Jesus did, that's why:

> Behold, I send you out as sheep in the midst of wolves. Therefore be wise as serpents and harmless as doves (Matthew 10:16).

As Christian creatives, it is our job to be like the serpent and the dove at the same time. Why is the serpent subtle? Why is it slow moving, and why does it approach its target with great caution? Because it's learning, that's why. It's learning the methods and behaviors of its intended target, and that's what we have to do as well: Learn about our target. We must become educated about our goal.

What industry are you trying to break into? You must learn all you can about it. Read about it. Study it. Ask others who work in that industry. Shadow other people and see how to behave in that industry. There is no simple way in. Some folks might make it look like there is, but trust me, they've studied and learned just like you need to do. The serpent doesn't rush, and neither should we. A lot of us think there's a "get rich quick" scheme out there that is just waiting for us to find it, but that is simply incorrect. Success will come with learning, patience, and waiting until the time is right to strike at the opportunity.

Yet, at the same time, we need to be like the dove: peaceful, tranquil, hopeful. We must not be ones to stir up strife, confusion, and disorder. Don't freak out and make things difficult for yourself and others as you approach the target. Learn as you go, be committed and focused like the serpent, but have a peaceful and hopeful air about you as you do so. You'll very quickly find that you'll attract far more allies and supporters with this approach. Plus, you won't raise the level of your blood pressure along the way.

Remember: Jesus is on your side. There is nothing He tells you that's designed to hurt you.

Be wise yet peaceful. That is a winning combination.

# Time

Buying things. Selling things. This is what makes the world go 'round. Without commerce and business transactions, there really would be no need for you to have a job or make money. Without commerce and business transactions, you wouldn't even have a way to spend money if you had it. Business and money are just facts of life. We need to exchange things so someone will give us money—so we can buy food, shelter, and clothing.

But what will we exchange for the money?

For many of us, *time* is what we exchange. That's our most valuable commodity. We only have a certain amount per day, and we can't make any more of it. We give our bosses forty hours of our time per week, and in return, we get a certain amount of money we can use to live. But when we exchange that time for a job we aren't satisfied with or a job we feel we aren't supposed to be doing any longer, then it can seem like a huge waste of our most valuable and irreplaceable commodity.

As creatives, we need to learn time management, and we need to learn it now. Why? Because with proper time management and proper scheduling, you'll be more productive and able to accomplish more of the vision God has given you. And once you're more productive, you'll feel a sense of accomplishment, which will increase your confidence overall.

Time management can be hard for some people. If it's not something you're accustomed to, then you need to do yourself a favor and become accustomed to it. If it's scary, it shouldn't be. Time management or scheduling NEEDS to become a part of your lifestyle. Without it, we allow ourselves to let things slide and procrastinate until it's too late to fix them.

But how can we become better at time management? What does it take to start thinking in a more organized way?

>#1: The desire to do so.

>#2: a renewed mind

>#3: the willingness to be uncomfortable for a short time

*Wow,* you may be thinking, *that all seems pretty intense.* Well, it is. You want to see your vision come to pass, right? You want to be successful, right? Time management is essential to making this all happen. Let's go over each item one at a time.

## The Desire to Do So

*And He shall give you the desires of your heart (Psalm 37:4).*

To make anything at all happen in our lives, there must be a desire for it to happen. Good things, things that last, do not happen instantly or accidentally. They need to be made to happen, and most importantly, they need to be made to happen by you. Your decisions affect not only you, but all those around you. You have desired to do many things in life. If you want to begin learning time management, then desiring it is a very important thing. You need to set your mind on wanting to become better at time management, and you'll start to see the Lord move you in that direction.

## The Renewed Mind

*Be transformed by the renewing of the mind (Romans 12:2).*

We all think a certain way. Our mindset is determined by many factors. If you're a young person, your mindset is more easily altered. If you're an older person, it seems like it's much more difficult to change, but change IS possible. However, again, the change must be desired. But once the decision is made, then the mind must be renewed.

A renewed mind will transform you and change circumstances in your life. Thinking a certain way can not only change your life for the better, it can also change your life for the worse. The decision is up to you. We can choose to eat cake or go to the gym. Both yield different results, but results will come no matter what. And the decisions we make now not only affect us, but will affect our families for years to come. If you're a person who isn't great at time management, then begin renewing your mind to the idea that you could be a very organized and scheduled type of person. Pray about it and see how the Lord will begin to move you in that direction.

## The Willingness to Be Uncomfortable for a Short Time

*"Have I not commanded you? Be strong and of good courage; do not be afraid, nor be dismayed, for the Lord your God is with you wherever you go" (Joshua 1:9).*

The problem with the world these days (man, I sure sound like an old person here, don't I?) is that people expect everything in life to be easy and all success must come without one ounce of effort or discomfort.

Jesus didn't die so we could be comfortable. He died to save our souls. Now, He doesn't WANT us to be uncomfortable, but He DOES want us to be warriors. And warriors fight.

*"You did not choose me, but I chose you and appointed you that you should go and bear fruit and that your fruit should abide, so that whatever you ask the Father in my name, he may give it to you" (John 15:16 ESV).*

Jesus tells us in that verse to "bear fruit." You can't get fruit unless you plant a tree, and planting a tree—tending to it, watering it, pruning it, harvesting the fruit—takes work and a lot of it. Then, if you plan on selling the fruit, that takes work, too. Jesus wants us working and learning constantly. Why?

Because it makes us stronger. And stronger Christians—more knowledgeable Christians—make better warriors and scare the heck out of the enemy.

Think about it: Who is the devil more likely to go after? The strong one or the weak one? Obviously, the weak one. We DO NOT want to be the weak one.

We all think that things should be super easy 100 percent of the time, but that's just not going to happen. If you want your project— your vision, your heart's desire—to come to pass, you need to be brave enough to get yourself strong even if it means being uncomfortable for a time.

If you want to get stronger, you need to lift weights. If you want to be a pro ball player, you practice. If you want to be a chef, you break eggs. Effort or sweat equity must be put into whatever it is we are doing. But when we sweat, we are usually doing something that's physically uncomfortable: working out, cleaning something, lifting something heavy, etc. The discomfort only lasts for a short time, but the results can last for a lifetime.

Get comfortable with being uncomfortable. It will keep your mind sharp, and you'll be ready and willing to take on more challenges.

Do you want results, or do you want to stay in the comfort zone?

These three disciplines will most definitely help you become a master of your own time. We have to start managing time, and there's no better time to start doing so than today.

Think I put the word 'time' in there enough?

# Day One!

*Who [with reason] despises the day of small things (beginnings)? (Zechariah 4:10 AMP).*

You have to start somewhere, right?

This can be a happy day or a terrifying one. The choice is yours. After all, it's the day you've been waiting for, right?! This is the day you start building your dream into the reality you know it can be. And as exciting as that can be, it comes with a huge dose of reality. You know you need to acquire the resources and people necessary to make this ship float (especially if your dream is to build a ship!).

All jokes aside. Now, you need to make a list of what to do on day one. (Follow this list every day and add to it as you go. You will see that different needs pop up every day as you begin to travel down the road toward your goal.)

1. What is the most important thing I can do today? Is it a phone call? An online search? Is it designing a logo? Hiring that first person? Starting a new bank account? What is it?

2. What am I CAPABLE of doing today? What you WANT to do today and what you are CAPABLE of doing today are two entirely different things. Listen, we all want to have a million people order our product online, but are you set up right now to fulfill 1 million orders? How about a 100,000? How about 10,000? How about 10? Do you even have a website set up yet? Now is the time to do whatever it is you are capable of doing no matter how

small it seems. If all you can do right now is post an Instagram photo about your dream, then that is what you do. It helps build a connection to your goal. Trust me, every effort adds up.

3. How many hours a day do you put into this? This is important. You need to devote time—every day—to your goal. No question. The amount of hours is up to you. But remember, no one is going to care about your dream as much as you, so you will be putting in the most hours at the outset until you can build your team around you.

4. What resources do you need at this point? Start compiling things now, even if it's one or two things. But start building your supply of resources ASAP.

5. What connections do you have that could help you along? (You could actually file this part under *resources* as well, but sometimes social connections are considered separate from physical resources although it is definitely okay to combine the two.) Do you have family? Friends? Work associates? Church associates? Any rich relatives out there? Who do you know that you could talk to about your dream? Who could help you? This is an important thing to think about. Remember, we talked about the Good Samaritan having connections, right? Now is the time to see which ones you have. It is all part of your ultimate goal.

6. Stay motivated! Easier said than done, right? On day one, it's super easy to stay motivated! You're just getting started! It's go time! You're fired up! But as the days, weeks, and months come and go, it's going to be up to you to keep yourself excited about the dream. Sometimes, you may be the only one who is. But if you

can make this commitment to yourself on day one, it will be much easier to stay excited down the road when things get a bit more challenging.

## List Some Tasks You Can Complete on Day One:

1.

2.

3.

# Obstacles and Steps

You knew this was coming, huh? I mean, c'mon, with any great endeavor come the inevitable stumbling blocks or *obstacles*. They come in all shapes and sizes: people, location, finances, resources, time. Seriously, you know the drill. It seems like everything we try to do is met with some kind of challenge, obstacle, or limitation. What's the deal? Can't we ever get a break?

(Insert frustrated scream here.)

Okay. Now that that's over let's get real. Yes, obstacles pop up. Yes, challenges occur. Yes, it's hard to get the plane off the ground sometimes, but I have news for you: You're NOT a TYPICAL creative person! You have Jesus Christ as your Lord and Savior! He's the very same Savior who said you could speak to the mountain, and it would be moved and thrown into the sea (see Mark 11:23).

Last time I looked, a mountain could be considered an obstacle. Jesus said that we could speak to it or deal with it so that very obstacle would be removed from our path.

There was a guy named Moses who freed a bunch of his people from Egyptian bondage and then found himself at the edge of the Red Sea with seemingly no escape from the Egyptian warriors that were pursuing them. But Moses trusted the Lord, and the Lord parted the Red Sea, and they walked to freedom (see Exodus 14). (Oh, and the Egyptians drowned in the process, too.)

Now, you may not have a literal Red Sea or actual mountain in front of you, but when you're pursuing a dream, sometimes ANY obstacle—any hindrance at all—can seem just as big as either one of those.

"But, Butch," you're asking, "how do I overcome those obstacles? How do I not only overcome them, but how do I overcome the NEXT one and the next and the next? WHY IS ALL THIS SO HARD?"

First of all, calm down. Yes, this is hard, but EVERYTHING is hard. IT DOESN'T NEED TO BE HARDER, though, THAN IT'S SUPPOSED TO BE! Let's look at my art career for a moment. When I was 15 years old, living in Michigan (which is exactly 1,000,000 miles away from the entertainment business in Hollywood), I knew I wanted to be an animator for the Walt Disney Studios. I wanted it so bad I could taste it. I was a kid who drew, and I loved art, was a huge animation nerd, and very much wanted to be part of it all. But when I looked at the level of art that the Disney Studios guys were putting out—the actual animation, background paintings, music, talent, not to mention the millions of toys, movies, TV shows, and theme parks—it was, in a word, SUPER-OVERWHELMING! How was a kid like me, a kid in his bedroom in Michigan, EVER going to get into a company like that? And a company that was located in California, by the way? And even if I could get there, how was I going to get them to notice me? And, most importantly, how was I ever going to get them to HIRE ME? (This story has a funny/ironic ending, so hang on.)

The simple answer to all the above questions is this: ONE STEP AT A TIME.

Let's look at all the obstacles that were in my way as I pursued my dream of becoming a professional artist. Remember: I had no road map, really. No exact blueprint. No crystal ball. I couldn't see the future, and I wasn't a billionaire. I was a normal teenage kid with a desire, with a dream.

*I wasn't even a Christian at this time.* (That is a story I will touch on later. I did not receive the Lord until I was 35 years old. Before that, I was a completely unsaved, secular person.)

But here is what I was facing and how I achieved my dream one step at a time.

## Obstacle 1: Getting to California

I lived in Michigan. When I was a kid, Michigan could not have been farther away from Hollywood and the animation business. Talk about an obstacle! How do you even GET to Hollywood when you live in the Midwest? I didn't have any connections in Hollywood, and no one in my family had ever been in the entertainment biz which was located in sunny California. So how was I going to get there? I would need a way in. So, when I was 16 years old, I found a college in California called the California Institute of the Arts (Cal Arts), and guess what? They had a Character Animation program that was taught by a lot of former Disney artists! How cool was that? I could be taught by former Disney artists, get to know them, have connections with them, AND be in California to boot? No way!

I found a way into California. Step one completed.

All I had to do next was get into the school.

## Obstacle 2: Getting into the School

I had to work on my portfolio. I had looked into the school's requirements, and they required a top-notch portfolio. Now, I was a decent artist at the time though I was very young, but I was certainly not at a level I would call "Disney level." I knew it would require a lot of work, so about two years before I would be out of high school (I was a sophomore at that time), I began to slowly develop my art skills in any way that I could. That meant I drew, and I drew, and I drew in any and every style I could think of. I knew I had to learn a lot of "life drawing" (drawing objects, animals, and people from real life), so I would go to the Detroit Zoo and draw the animals. I would even go during the winter because, since it was freezing outside, it was free to get in. Sometimes I think I was the ONLY customer in the zoo at that time! But I learned and I improved over the next two years. When I was 18 (I was a senior in high school by that time), I submitted my portfolio to Cal Arts. Right before I graduated high school, I got the great news that I had been accepted!

All that hard work over the previous two years had paid off.

Step two completed.

## Obstacle 3: Paying for the School

Hooray! I had achieved what I had perceived was going to be the biggest obstacle: getting accepted into Cal Arts! As with any dream, once one victory was realized, another challenge arose. This is clearly indicated in the Bible:

*"To whom much is given, from him much will be required" (Luke 12:48).*

Yes. Much was required. The money to now PAY for the school was needed. How was I going to do this? The tuition at that time (this was 1983 … time flies!) was $10,000 a year! For a kid like me, at that time, it may as well have been a million dollars. So, what did I do? Did I say, "Well, forget it. I worked super hard for two years to get accepted, and now I have to give up because I don't have the money?"

Absolutely not! I wasn't about to let a little thing like money turn me back. *(Side note here: see, when we can view obstacles like money as little things, they lose their power over us and allow us to step over them.)* I did the thing a lot of college-bound students do: I applied for financial aid. Yes, it was a loan, but at the time, it was an option that I was willing to pursue because nothing mattered more to me then than getting into that school. So, with a lot of financial help from my dad (thank God for him) and the financial aid, I found myself able to pay for my first year.

Step three completed!

## Obstacle 4: Paying Back the Loan

I'm jumping ahead a bit here because we need to talk about the importance of paying back a loan. I bring this up because, as a Christian creative, it is vital that we try to stay out of debt as much as possible. I'm not saying that our lives will always be debt free or that sometimes issues occur where only a loan from someone will solve the problem, BUT I am saying that if we get into debt, ever, it is very important we have a mindset of repaying it as quickly as possible. In my case, that financial aid I told you I applied for, well, I went to Cal Arts for three years, and I had to take a loan out every year. And the tuition increased every year as well. So, my first year cost $10,000, but each year after cost about $13,000, and then $15,000. By the time I was done with three years of school, I owed the loan institution about $38,000. Now, this was in 1986 dollars (the year I left school and got into the workforce), so it was a massive debt for me. Did I turn away from it, though? Did I just not pay it and let the loan institution come after me?

No. I paid back every cent of that loan. It took me over ten years, but I paid it back with installments of about $50 a month. There were many months, as I started making more and more money, that I was able to double and triple the amounts I paid, but eventually, the loan was paid back. I even took the debt into my marriage when I got married in 1992, and my wife understood that this was something that needed to be done. Bless her!

Step four completed.

*(The payback of a financial debt can be a HUGE obstacle if you allow it to be. But, just like working at getting into the school, I had to pay back this debt one step at a time. You can do it, too. No matter if it's a debt, a plan, a dream, a desire, or anything else, you can overcome any and all obstacles one step at a time).*

## Obstacle 5: Getting into the Animation Business

It was definitely 'go' time. I had just completed three years of schooling at the most prestigious animation/art school in the country, I had made a great many connections through all the awesome animation and art teachers who came through Cal Arts, and I was told, right before I left school: "Congratulations on your achievement. Now you will have to begin paying back your student loan." These words rang heavy in my ears for sure. I knew I was talented but definitely not the most talented artist out there. Yet I also understood that I had improved and learned so much in that school. The animation business is a great business, but it is a SMALL business compared to so many others. There are jobs available but not millions of jobs just ready for the taking. It was and still is a very competitive business. If you're an artist—and it REALLY helps if you're a good one—you have to do one very important thing: HUSTLE. You not only must be talented, but you have to hustle for every connection and every opportunity. Animation jobs are just like any other jobs: People want them, and there aren't very many of them.

Long story short, I hustled. I got employment and used each and every job and every position to further educate myself, increasing my talent and position.

Step five completed.

## Obstacle 6: Getting Fired and Bouncing Back

Oh yeah, I forgot to include this part. I got fired once! It was terrible. It was right at the beginning of my career, too! I was at a job—an animation job, one of my first—and I was thrilled to be there, but I simply couldn't do this one aspect of the job they asked me to do. In my defense— which isn't much of one—I was hired to do another aspect of the job, but once I got there, they switched me to a department I was untrained for, especially at the speed they needed it. I was soon let go. It was devastating. I don't know if this has ever happened to you, but if it has, you know the feeling.

I had two choices: give up and go back to Michigan or suck it up and look for another job.

Guess what I did? Yep. I looked for another job, and thankfully, I got one. I made myself learn to do the task I had been let go for and was able to get employment elsewhere in the animation industry. I had worked too hard to get into the industry and was not about to stop then. YOU NEED TO KNOW THAT SOMETIMES BEING FORCED TO CHANGE JOBS—change environments—CAN BE A GOOD THING!

Step six completed.

## A Key Factor

Here is a VERY KEY FACTOR I need to tell you: During all this, in the year 2000, I got saved and invited Jesus Christ to be my Lord and my Savior. It was the greatest decision I have ever made, and my life changed from that point on. Jesus was able to show me—now that I had worldly experience and worldly success–that He could direct my heart and my efforts into working for Him and His Kingdom, helping others embrace the truth that we live in a fallen world and it is only through Him that we can achieve real success and achieve things we never thought possible.

I found out through Christ that I was more than just an artist. I was a storyteller, I was a director, I was a producer, and ultimately, I was a show creator. I was someone who wasn't just seeking employment. I could become someone who could actually GIVE the employment.

Step seven completed.

Now you see that, every part of this VERY, VERY CONDENSED VERSION of my journey became a reality because I did each and every part of it ONE STEP AT A TIME. And I PRAISE GOD that I found Jesus in the process.

Anyone can take one step. The first step. Especially you.

Don't look at the millions of steps ahead. Just focus on the one that's right in front of you. Then take the next one, then the next. There may be days, weeks, even months, or years between steps, but take them anyway! Your journey begins "with a single step" as the old saying goes.

And I want to remind you that I started off doing all of that BEFORE I was even a Christian. I did not have the ability to access the God-given authority I had waiting for me because I did NOT have the Lord living inside my heart at the time. I was as worldly as they come and then some. And I was STILL able to do all of that. This is not to brag or boast at all, far from it. I am merely telling you all this to illuminate how, if a WORLDLY, UNSAVED, UNWASHED person like I was could do that, simply living by my wits and under my own strength, imagine what my journey would have been like had I allowed Jesus into my heart all those years ago. I would have made different decisions, had different friends, and had many different experiences. However, like Paul the apostle, I was called into the ministry later in life and given the chance to testify about the glory of Christ and how much He influences my work, my family, my life, and all my choices. I am forever grateful of the life I had before Jesus—warts and all—but I am exceptionally grateful of the current life I am now experiencing.

Taking steps. Hustling. Making connections. These rules hold true for ANY profession, not just the animation industry. That's what I was gifted to do.

What are YOU gifted to do?

Oh, and by the way, ironically, I never ended up working for Disney Studios! I went to California to work there and ended up working for a lot of other studios, all in the television category. Nickelodeon is where I ended up spending most of my career. Interesting how following one dream—in my case, the Disney dream—can lead to realizing so many other dreams. So, keep in mind that God can use anything to help you achieve your desires—even if your desires take you through a bunch of other desires until you reach the goal!

It's up to you to simply take one step at a time.

## What Are Some Key Obstacles You Need to Overcome?

# Flexibility

Much depends on your ability to be flexible. You must be able to listen to God as you take your journey. Stability is important, yes, but you can't be so rooted in the "one way" of doing things that you don't listen to new ideas and take advice from others who may have valuable insight to your situation. The worst thing we can ever do is get into pride and begin to believe that our way is the only way and that we don't need to grow or change.

*The Lord detests all the proud of heart. Be sure of this: They will not go unpunished (Proverbs 16:5 NIV).*

To be in pride or arrogance is the surest and quickest way to failure. Many people think they have everything all figured out and don't need anyone else to help them. But that is very far from the truth. When I was working in the Hollywood animation industry making high-level television cartoons, it was definitely a very difficult thing to do. I most certainly could not do it on my own. I needed a very large team to help get everything completed. I needed everyone, including  artists, writers, musicians, actors, and editors. They were all super creative people who all had skill and vision, but in the end, I was the one who made the final decisions. Can you imagine how much work it would have been if I had had so much pride that I refused to let anyone else do any of the work? If I had been so insistent on making it all "mine" that I refused to hear the opinions of anyone else or listen to anyone else's ideas?

That would have been a disaster. Instead, it was so much better to have creative ideas and amazing work come from the team I had. It not only made the shows great, but it helped me tremendously and empowered the entire team.

Imagine being a quarterback on a football team and trying to play the whole game by yourself! You'd get exhausted and probably not be able to play again for a while. Maybe one game a year? Instead of that scenario, make sure you take advantage of your team. Empower those around you and those working with you to use their skills to move the ball down the field. This way you'll conserve your energy, grow, and learn. Allow your team to use their skills and get the vision to its intended goal.

In the Bible, Peter gave a great example of being flexible. In the book of Luke, the story is told of Peter (known as Simon at the time) working in a way he wasn't used to, but he did it anyway:

*When He had stopped speaking, He said to Simon, "Launch out into the deep and let down your nets for a catch." But Simon answered and said to Him, "Master, we have toiled all night and caught nothing; nevertheless at Your word I will let down the net." And when they had done this, they caught a great number of fish, and their net was breaking. So they signaled to their partners in the other boat to come and help them. And they came and filled both the boats, so that they began to sink. When Simon Peter saw it, he fell down at Jesus' knees, saying, "Depart from me, for I am a sinful man, O Lord!" For he and all who were with him were astonished at the catch of fish which they had taken (Luke 5:4–9).*

Peter had worked all night in the way he knew how. He did things the way he had always done things, and it wasn't working. And here came this guy Jesus telling him to throw his net into the water anyway, despite the fact Peter had caught nothing in that area.

Peter had two choices: He could tell Jesus, "Thanks but no thanks. Been there done that. I know more about fishing than You do. After all, I'm a professional fisherman." Or he could have done what he did: throw in his net anyway because Jesus told him to. Thank goodness, Peter listened to Jesus because Peter was rewarded with the biggest catch of fish he had ever caught! Peter was willing to be flexible and listen as opposed to being arrogant and stubborn and demanding it all be done his way.

What is the Lord telling YOU to do now?

Be ready to pivot when the moment calls for it. Yes, having a strong vision is vital. That sets the goalpost for where everyone is heading, but make sure you're not so rooted and unmoving that you can't dodge out of the way when an obstacle pops up.

## What Are Some Areas Where You Can See Yourself Being More Flexible?

1.

2.

3.

# Staying Motivated

Day one of the Big Dream is easy! You're pumped! You're ready to go! You're on fire! Everyone is patting you on the back and singing your praises, saying, "Go for it! You can do it!" It's a grand time as people watch your boat set sail, wave to you from the dock, and throw confetti. You're on top of the world, and you just know it's all going to be smooth sailing from here. What could possibly go wrong?

Well, for starters, big dreams don't always happen overnight. There will be many days, weeks, months, and years spent moving toward your desired goal. You want to sell chocolate chip cookies and get them on the shelves of a major retailer? You're going to need a ton of cookies, a ton of chips, and a ton of connections to the cookie manufacturers and the retail buyers. You're going to need a marketing team and a distribution network.

In short, you're going to need a lot. And this goes for any dream no matter what size.

So, considering all this, how do we keep the fires of motivation burning when the cheering stops and the real work kicks in?

Let's look at what the Bible says about staying motivated:

*Therefore encourage one another and build each other up, just as in fact you are doing (1 Thessalonians 5:11 NIV).*

"Build each other up." Having people around you who can encourage you is a key factor.

## List the Names of People in Your Life Who Can Be Constant Sources of Encouragement:

*You can include yourself, but you need to include other people.*

What else does the Bible say about encouragement?

*And let us consider how we may spur one another on toward love and good deeds, not giving up meeting together, as some are in the habit of doing, but encouraging one another—and all the more as you see the Day approaching (Hebrews 10:24–25 NIV).*

We have to encourage one another. Yes, it is vital that people encourage us, BUT it is super important that WE encourage others as well. If we want encouragement, we need to be people who GIVE encouragement.

*Do not be deceived, God is not mocked; for whatever a man sows, that he will also reap (Galatians 6:7–9).*

Motivation is not an easy thing to find for some people, yet accomplishing ANYTHING in life takes a great many components coming together. Without motivation, nothing will ever get done. Think of having all the pieces you need to build a car. Everything is there: the wheels, the body, the engine, the lights, the electronics. Everything is included. But if there's no motivation on the part of the builder, then all the pieces will sit there as an unrealized vision.

Understand that motivation is completely up to you. You can have the world's biggest cheering section around you, but all they can do is cheer for you. You're the one who has to lace up the shoes and run the race. It's your dream. Your goal. You care the most about it.

You need to become a motivated person if you're not already. Remember: As a Christian creative, you have the Lord with you always. Jesus is a master motivator, so let Him motivate you.

Let's look at some folks in the Bible who needed to be motivated and the Lord showed up for them:

1. Noah was motivated to build a giant ark because God told him to. It took him over 100 years! You can bet he had to stay motivated!

2. Moses was motivated by God to free the Hebrews from Egyptian bondage even though Moses was unconvinced he could do it.

3. David was motivated to stop Goliath because he knew God was with him.

4. Joseph was motivated to continue on even though his brothers left him for dead, he was accused of a crime, and he was going to die in prison. But he eventually became ruler of Egypt!

5. Esther was motivated to stand up against the slaughter of her people even though it could have meant her own death.

History could have been completely different had these people (and many others) not been motivated. Think about it: ANYONE you have ever been influenced by was a motivated individual who accomplished something. It takes motivation, and it takes YOU deciding to move. And you must do it every day.

Our biblical friends found motivation. You can, too.

**List the Names of People, Things, or Activities That Can Keep You Motivated:**

1.

2.

3.

4.

5.

# You Are a Green Banana

*"For the earth yields crops by itself: first the blade, then the head, after that the full grain in the head" (Mark 4:28).*

Nothing worthwhile happens instantly. Think about that. Whenever something affects us instantly, it's usually not good for us. Drugs and alcohol, for example, affect us instantly, but we all know that the effects are very temporary. If we aren't careful, however, they can lead to long-term negative issues.

You're a green banana. You're on your way to becoming ripe.

Things that matter—things that will last—take time to grow and get established. Newsflash: Your dream will not become a reality overnight. I'm sure you already knew that, but it needed to be said anyway. If your dream happens overnight, it most likely won't last. It's like one of the seeds in the parable of the sower in Matthew 13:1–23, more specifically, like the seed that is sown in the stony places:

*"But he who received the seed on stony places, this is he who hears the word and immediately receives it with joy; yet he has no root in himself, but endures only for a while. For when tribulation or persecution arises because of the word, immediately he stumbles" (Matthew 13:20–21).*

This parable talks about different seeds sown into different types of ground. We all know that various seeds produce various results based on what type of ground they're planted in, correct? Well, the same goes for your goals and ideas. Each idea must be nurtured in the proper environment with the right types of influence. For example, if you're trying to sell baby clothes, you don't sell them at an auto parts store. There are specific items you sell at an auto parts store, and you need to be aware of which environment is best for your idea to grow.

And *grow* is a key word there. Your vision will not be fully realized overnight. That is just a fact. If God gave you everything all at once at the exact time you asked for it, then it would most likely kill you or at the very least disable you. You simply wouldn't be able to handle it. You need training in many areas before each and every aspect of your dream becomes a reality. This is the "blade, ear and full corn in the ear" part—the growth part. Nobody wants to eat a green banana. It's not ripe yet. It's ON ITS WAY to being ripe, but there are still a lot of things that must happen before it's ready.

You are that green banana. You are full of potential and on your way to ripening.

When I was first starting out working in the animation industry, I was 21 years old, and I began my professional career as a character designer. This meant that I would design new characters for all the shows I worked on, kind of like a casting director for a TV show or movie. In a live action project, they would find actors to portray roles, and in the animation world, I would draw characters to portray roles. It was a great job! I learned a lot, but it was only one very small part of what it takes to build an entire animated cartoon, whether it's a series or a movie.

Fourteen years later at the age of 35, I finally got to produce and run my own animated shows, meaning I was in charge of EVERY ASPECT of the shows from the character designs to the scripts, to the voice recordings, to the music to the final edit, and so on. But back when I first started, there was simply NO WAY I could have handled all the responsibility necessary to complete a task like that. It took not only a growth in my level of skill as an artist and storyteller, but growth as a man. I had to learn many things. I had gotten married, had a home, started to have children, learned how to handle money better, and learned how to, basically, be a better adult. Had I received my own shows at age 21, there was simply no way I would have been mentally ready to handle the job successfully.

I was a green banana getting riper all the time. The process was moving and changing me, but I didn't realize it until later. The one thing I NEVER did was give up. And you will get through your process, too, as long as you don't give up.

You may have just now started down the road to your dream, or you may be well on your way and have already learned a lot. But the process is the process. God is protecting you because that's what He does.

It's like going to a gym, and on day one, you think you can lift 200 pounds over your head with absolutely no strength training at all. That's foolish. You're going to hurt yourself. You need to start by lifting 20 pounds, then 50, then 100, and so forth. If you stick with it, pretty soon you'll get stronger and stronger.

It's the moving through the process that trains us how to handle our success once it comes. God is all about strong roots and foundations growing FIRST before the fruit starts appearing. So, as you move into your dream, don't despise the process. God is not trying to make it hard on you. He is guiding you through the gauntlet so you can get stronger.

Remember: The process is threefold:

1. The blade (just starting)

2. The ear (you can see growth but still have a way to go)

3. The full corn in the ear (moving in your desired goal and producing fruit)

## What Part of the Process Are in Right Now?

Be as descriptive as possible:

# Enhancing Your Skill Set

I got fired.

I know I just mentioned it in the previous chapter, but I wanted to get your attention.

I was fired from my very first professional job as a cartoonist. I had worked so hard to get to that job. I had left Michigan, gotten into art school, worked hard to hone my craft, found this job, and was so excited to finally be given the chance to do what I had dreamed of doing.

Then, just a few weeks in, I was let go. Why?

Because, as I stated before, I couldn't do the task I was given.

Now, as a brief explanation, I was hired to do a certain job, a job I was pretty good at. Knew it well. You might say it was my chief skill. But the first week I came into the job, they gave me an assignment I was untrained for. Now, in this situation, I had two choices:

1. I could refuse to do the job. But how would that be received? I would be looked at as difficult and a quitter. Plus, it would make me look unsure.

2. I could give it a shot. At least this way I would look like a team player, right? And appear more confident, right?

Either way, it didn't work out. I failed at the new assignment because I wasn't trained for it, and I was fired. Besides the hurt and inner humiliation (hey, no one wants to get fired), I took one other very important piece of knowledge with me: I needed to enhance my skill set. I needed to get better at other things instead of the one particular thing I was hired for. Yes, I was very good at that task. However, had I been able to effectively perform the other task, I would never have been let go.

I realized that, to stay in the profession I had worked so hard to get into, I would need to become a more valuable artist. Sort of a "Swiss Army Knife" of artists, if you will. Basically, I made a promise to myself that I would become so versatile that, no matter what studio I worked for, I would be able to draw whatever or perform whatever task they asked me to do. So, I set out to do that. I found other jobs, but I worked hard during off hours to get more experience, studying more and making myself learn all I could. Within a few years, I had gone from "the guy who did that ONE thing well" to "the guy who could do A LOT OF THINGS well." This instantly made me more valuable and increased my paycheck along the way.

You need to do this, too. It won't happen overnight, but you need to become good at more than one thing. You may be great at playing guitar, but learn the drums, too. Learn the saxophone, the piano. Heck, learn the xylophone! Whatever makes you more valuable, LEARN IT!

When you become more valuable, you become an ASSET. Something necessary. An important tool that is needed to make everything work. You go from being TOLERATED to APPRECIATED. MAKE SURE TO ENHANCE AND INCREASE YOUR SKILL SET! Get better at everything!

## What Are Some Things You Can Learn (or Do More of) to Enhance Your Skill Set?

*List in order of importance.*

1.

2.

3.

# Growth and Responsibility

If you're enhancing your skill set, becoming a more valuable asset, then you are going to grow. No doubt about it. It's inevitable. You'll get a better job. You'll get promoted. You'll be given more responsibility. It will all come as a result of the hard work, time, and sacrifice you've put in. It's just a byproduct of all that effort and increased learning on your part. But once the growth comes, once you get more responsibility, how do you handle that?

What does the Bible say?

*"To whom much is given, from him much will be required"* (Luke 12:48).

This is Jesus saying to us that, when given many things (responsibilities), much will be required from us. Things like time, effort, and sacrifice. You may be one of those people who instantly understands this concept. You're hard-working, responsible—it all comes second nature to you. But you'd be very surprised (or perhaps you wouldn't be surprised) that there are a great many people who have no concept of this at all. They live with a false sense of reality. They believe that simply by wanting something it will magically appear for them. Then they complain and get upset when it doesn't show up.

Or, if it does show up, somehow, they are dumbfounded when they can't maintain what they have been given and are stunned when they lose it all.

There are many examples of this phenomenon, but a simple one that comes to mind is a person who wins the lottery. Let's say someone is extremely poor most of their life. They've never really made any money or been able to own anything. They're in debt and have a tough time paying their rent. A tough life for sure. Now, let's say they buy a lottery ticket and manage to actually win 50 million dollars!

Wow! 50 million! Can you imagine? What an incredible thing. This person has now gone from one of the poorest people around to one of the richest in a matter of moments. They have been GIVEN 50 million dollars. A truly life-changing turn of events has happened. Question: What do you think will happen to this person?

Odds are they will lose the money and end up deeper in debt than ever before. And why would this happen? Because handling 50 million dollars properly REQUIRES a lot of training and expertise! For example, what bank would they put the money in? What are the fees? What are the interest rates? How much interest can you make on 50 million and in what timeframe?

Are they going to buy stocks? Which ones? How much? And who is going to monitor this? The stock market is not for amateurs.

If they buy something (like a house for their family, for example), do they buy it outright with cash, or do they get a mortgage? What are the terms and/or payments involved?

Do they want to invest in other ways? Money market accounts? IRAs? Real estate rentals? ALL of this takes training and expertise, and this person has none because they have never been able to manage 500 dollars, let alone 50 million.

Most likely, they have a year or two of fun with the money, spend too much, and give too much to family and friends. Then, let's say they have a moment of clarity and try to invest but have no idea how to do so and get into a bad business deal or two. This ends up costing more money. Pretty soon, they are out of money, have more bills to pay, and no one can come to their rescue. They have failed because, even though they were GIVEN a lot of money, they didn't have what was REQUIRED to maintain it.

The same thing can happen to us as we pursue our goal. If we are given too much too fast, without the proper training and experience, we will end up losing all the things we are trying to build. We serve a good God. A God who loves us! He's not going to give you the keys to a Ferrari when you've never even driven a tricycle. God is patient and kind. He wants the best for us all and wants us to succeed! He knows that, as we build creative muscle, we will get stronger along the way and more knowledgeable. We will become more skilled so that, when the big moment comes, when it's time to step through that doorway, we'll be ready and won't collapse as the new weight of responsibility is placed upon us.

We live in a time where things can happen instantly. If we want something, it is very easy to get nowadays. You don't even need to leave your chair in your home, and you can order anything with your phone, and it will show up for you ASAP. People will get fat liposuctioned off their body rather than do the physical exercise and dietary discipline needed to take the weight off naturally. They all want the cake that's pictured on the box of cake mix but are unwilling to break the eggs and stir the batter in a way that will make it happen.

There are problems and issues I can tackle now as a full-grown adult that I never could have tackled when I was a kid. The reason is that I wasn't ready back then. I wasn't trained or equipped. But I am now. Problems that seemed huge then are easy to solve now. But it didn't happen overnight. It happened gradually so God could ease me into the position I am now in. It will happen for you, too but don't rush the growth. It will come. Just learn along the way. Watch how much wiser you become. And be ready to do what is required when you are given more and more.

LIST SOME THINGS YOU'VE BEEN LEARNING ABOUT LATELY:

# How Do We Make Money Using Our Gifts?

We make money by selling things; that is, unless you've inherited a lot of money or you have a counterfeit money printing press in your basement. But, for the most part, people make money by exchanging their time or services for income.

When you work a 9 to 5 job, you make money because you are selling your time to an employer. Your employer, in turn, sells the product you are helping them to produce. When it comes to your own idea, you basically become your own employer. It's up to you to manage things, find customers, fill orders, and keep the books. Oh, and you also want to make a healthy profit, too. That's pretty important, huh?

You need to find a way to SELL your creativity to someone. When I was working in the Hollywood animation business for 35 years, I not only made a living doing exactly what I loved (drawing and writing stories for cartoons), but I also learned how to sell my talents to major studios so I could get paid. Yes, I started out working for other people and helping them with their ideas, but I ended up taking every opportunity that came along to sell my own ideas and began to become my own boss. And it eventually happened because I pursued it relentlessly.

I never gave up. You need to do that same thing: NEVER GIVE UP. I know that sounds like a big thing, but it is a necessary thing. Every single successful person you have ever heard of has spent a great deal of their time not giving up. They persisted despite the circumstances and obstacles that came against them. You are guaranteed to lose if you give up.

Have I said the words *give up* enough? Because I really wanted to stress that giving up is bad. Okay, great. So that's out of the way.

Back to the "selling" part. To make any kind of income using your gift, you are going to have to convince someone that your gift is valuable. Rock musicians do it all the time. People love their music, so they not only buy the albums, but they go to see the musicians in concert, too. There is a value placed upon their gift. Now, the musician probably didn't start out by getting paid. They probably started off by making no money at all. But as time went on and they didn't give up (notice I got another mention in there), they slowly and surely became more and more valuable as their music caught on.

The same can happen for you. But you must start at the beginning.

# Understanding the Marketplace

This is the goal. The big time. You want people to see what it is you've been working on all this time, and *the marketplace* is where they will see it. It's the place where people buy and sell or reject and pass over. The main goal is to get them to buy your product. Even if you want to give it away, you'll want them to love it so much they will want more and more of it.

The marketplace can be different things for different people. Yes, there is the traditional image of a market that we all have in our minds with shelves lined with jars, boxes, and other products. That's the physical marketplace. But there is also the *online* marketplace where you can buy anything in the blink of an eye. This requires a knowledge of online advertising or social media.

But how do we get our dream—our product—*into* the marketplace? How do we get it to a place where it can finally be consumed by all the consumers out there? As creatives, we are sometimes not as adept at selling as we are making the product itself. But this book exists so you can get some insight as to what's required of you and your team as you move forward into making your dream a reality.

If you're a creative Christian, then you understand the importance of sowing and reaping. You get back what you put in. The harvest is amazing. Everyone WANTS the harvest. But fewer people want to sow. It takes work to plow the field (doing research) and plant seeds (putting in the time and effort). If you're going to be a success in ANY field, you simply MUST put time into each step, so don't discount the importance of the go-to market strategy. It is vital.

## A GO-TO MARKET STRATEGY

This is exactly what it sounds like: a strategy on how to put your product on a marketplace "shelf" (whether physical or digital). If you want to be successful, I urge you to not simply open a lemonade stand on your front lawn and hope people stop by. Yes, you will get a few lookee-loos and some nice neighborhood folks who will buy your product out of kindness, some may even like it, but without a strategy or game plan, there is simply no way to create the necessary kind of interest or buzz around your idea to take it to the next level. Think about it: Does a winning football team ever take the field without a rock-solid plan of how they're going to play the game? No way. They think about every possible scenario that could happen on the field and then practice accordingly.

This may seem like an extremely daunting task—and it can be—but it needs to be done. Your plan for putting out a product must be taken seriously. Trust me, I have been on both ends of this situation, and planning things out is FAR better than just putting something out there and hoping people find it. The market is a HUGE place with many different options and possibilities, and unless you find a way to attract attention to YOUR product, you will get very easily lost in the shuffle.

The only way to plan a go-to market strategy is to understand the market and what you can expect. This will take research on your part.

Yes, I said a scary word: RESEARCH. A lot of creatives CAN'T STAND this word. To most, it means not being creative. Research sounds boring, tedious, and super time-consuming. But guess what?

It doesn't have to be. Research—studying and learning the lay of the land of the marketplace— is incredibly important and will make the difference between success and non-success. Think of it like this: You have a beautiful house. It's got beautiful shutters, beautiful landscaping, beautiful windows, doors, interior, pools, fountains, etc. The place, from the outside, looks incredible. BUT let's say there's no heater, no plumbing, and no electricity.

Still sound like a nice house? Sure, it's a HOUSE, but there's no guts, nothing that makes it comfortable to dwell in. It's like putting out a product with nothing behind it.

Sure, people like looking at the outside, but if there's no infrastructure—no research, no study of the market—then it may as well just be a shell of what it could be. Putting in the plumbing, electricity, and air conditioning may not be the pretty part, but if you don't have it, you may as well just have the icing and no cake.

STOPPING HERE TO SPEAK TO ALL THE CREATIVES WHO HAVE READ THIS FAR. Let's call this a "TIME TO ADDRESS THE AUDIENCE."

You've done well, Young Skywalker. You've come this far. You've managed to hear some real truths and maybe been given a new idea or two. For that and for staying the course so far, I want to say: NICE JOB!

HOWEVER (there's always a however, isn't there?), I want to take this moment to let you know that we are talking serious business here. Yes, I said business. This business that you are working hard to learn more about, this dream you have, this desire to do something creatively awesome could not only change your life for years to come, but it could change your family's life and your grandkids' lives for GENERATIONS. This is a very big deal you're undertaking, and it does NOT come for free. There is always a price to pay, and that price is—drum roll, please.....

DYING TO YOUR OLD WAY OF THINKING!

You can get free of your old mindset if you can be humble and admit that you need to learn. Jesus said,

*If anyone desires to come after Me, let him deny himself, and take up his cross, and follow Me (Matthew 16:24).*

The first part of that scripture is DENY YOURSELF! Basically, it's dying to yourself! LET HIM encourage you and give you the courage to move into areas that you've always felt uncomfortable about entering.

Yes, RESEARCH and DEVELOPMENT are hard sometimes. Yes, they're not super fun things to do—things we sometimes consider as non-creative—but listen: Everything you're going to do on your creative journey is going to be hard, at least at first. It will be hard until you do one very important thing: Change your mindset.

You need to get a new mindset about a great many things if you are going to be successful, starting with the idea that *successful people know how to do a lot of stuff!* And how did they learn to do a lot of stuff? Easy: THEY MADE THEMSELVES LEARN!

*The Bible says:*

*Be transformed by the renewing of your mind... (Romans 12:2).*

Jesus is all about renewing your mind. We MUST renew our minds if we are going to go on this journey.

Successful people didn't learn everything at once. Read that again. THEY DIDN'T LEARN EVERYTHING AT ONCE. This is good news and should take a lot of the pressure off you! YOU DON'T NEED TO LEARN IT ALL IN ONE DAY!

The learning comes after many weeks, months, and years of trial and error.

*GASP!* "You mean there will be errors, Butch?"

Shockingly, yes. There will be more errors than successes. But this happens to EVERYONE. There are ZERO exceptions.

Growing and shaping the old you into the new you that Christ knows you can be is what you're wanting to see happen. But if you keep a child's mindset and run from every challenge, you won't grow. You won't change.

Children don't do difficult things. They avoid them. Adults do things they don't want to do. Why? Because that is what adults do. I am not writing this book for children. I am writing to people who want to grow up and become strong, successful adults.

Here's something to remember: ADULTS GET RESULTS.

Remember, none of this is easy. This is why most creatives are never heard of: They can create something, but they can never figure out a way to get it noticed because it seems like too difficult a task. Listen: EVERYTHING is difficult the first time you try it. But keep trying, and you'll get better each time.

## Okay, Audience Address Over. Thanks for Reading. Now, Continuing...

If you're entering the market with a new brand of shoes, for example—*and we all know how many different kinds of shoe brands are out there, don't we?*—you need to understand the SHOE MARKET. Don't go poking your nose around in the FOOD MARKET because it doesn't apply to you (unless you have shoes made of food, which is a whole other story). But what is the shoe market like? Who are the big sellers? Who is your competition? Who are the manufacturers? Who are the designers? Who are the CUSTOMERS?

All these items as well as many more need to be considered and planned for as you prepare your amazing product for market. Your UNDERSTANDING of the market is a key factor in making your dream not only a reality, but a successful one at that. We all want to get things, but understanding or wisdom should be at the top of the list.

*In all your getting, get understanding (Proverbs 4:7).*

And this strategy may require others to come alongside you. It is very difficult to do anything of any value by yourself. Yes, it can be done, but if you have a team, you not only increase the odds of things increasing at a faster rate, but you also bless the people who come with you because they are also on the journey with you. Most of the time, as we start out, we have a bit of market understanding. More often than not, we are going to start a project in a market we already have an interest in like sports or comic books or cooking or whatever it may be. But it's important to increase that learning. We need to move from being a mere FAN of the market to being a PLAYER in the market. Ready to play? You need understanding to do it!

# Advertising

We've already talked about this a bit and how it's necessary, but let's talk about it more deeply. Doesn't matter HOW many ideas we have or how many goals we want to pursue, they make no difference unless they get SEEN and EMBRACED by other people. Period. This is key to the go-to market strategy.

Disneyland was just a thought until Walt Disney convinced other people—like bankers—to invest money into it. McDonald's was just another hamburger stand until the idea was presented in such a way to convince people that it was THE place to eat.

I wish there was one simple way to make it happen. The truth is that there are many ways to advertise a product in the marketplace, and here are a few:

1. Social media—Build a following on a social media platform and talk about your product constantly. (Once you post about a product you are, technically, introducing it into the marketplace. You're basically making your own TV commercial.)

2. Websites—Don't have one? Make one. Doesn't have to be fancy, but it's a landing spot where people can go to check you out. They are so easy to do now. Do it today.

3. Traditional media advertising—Television commercials, radio, billboards, newspaper ads, yes, these are still a thing. And they are still a great way to build awareness.

4. Email—Build an email list and send reminders to people all the time.

5. Word of mouth—Get people to talk about your product. Get them to talk to other people about your it. (This is called free advertising.)

These are the best ways to talk about what you have to offer. But even though people can become aware of your product, how will you get them to buy it? What will compel them to want what you are offering?

What problem are you solving for them? This is a key question. Your dream/goal/vision will only be a success if people want it, and they will only want it if it fills a need that they have.

## List Several Ways You Can Begin Advertising (Talking about) Your Product Today:

1.

2.

3.

4.

5.

Understanding the market only comes by getting into it. It is only through experience that our knowledge will increase. Think about it: You can read all about what it's like to be in a grocery store, but it's not until you actually walk in and experience all it has to offer will your knowledge grow.

Before you take your product out into the world, you need to know what the competition is like, too. Yes, believe it or not, there are other people out there with the same idea you have, and you have to look at what they have and what they are doing before you run out there and make a mistake. For example, you don't want to open a hamburger restaurant called McDonald's when you know very well that there is a multi-million-dollar company already in existence with that very name that is synonymous with hamburgers. You'll want to come up with a different name, at the very least, and make yourself as different from McDonald's as possible.

When I was working in the animation industry, I learned to do my homework before I pitched a new idea to a major studio. For example, if I knew a studio was making several different shows based on martial arts, the last thing I would ever do is bring them ANOTHER idea about martial arts. Even if I was convinced that my martial arts idea was the best martial arts idea EVER, I still wouldn't do it because, odds are, the studio was already filled to the brim with martial arts ideas, and the last thing they needed was another one. I would force myself to come up with an idea that was so different that the studio would have no choice but to make it happen.

This is where a creative—especially a Christian one with the mind of Christ—must push themselves to think of ideas that are different and unique. You need to think of ideas that are so special that they stand out from the crowd. I know it's not easy, and I know it's not something everyone can do, but if it were easy, then EVERYBODY would be doing it, right?

Think. Create. Make something happen. This is what you were born to do.

As creatives, we need to move our vision toward the marketplace. Whether it's a TV show you're making, a book you're writing, a song you're composing, a software company you're starting, or a ministry you're building, you know that it has to be different from everything else.

Let's use the hamburger example again: A hamburger is a hamburger, right? But there is a TON of hamburger restaurants out there, right? Same goes for cars, toothpaste, shoes, soda, coffee shops, etc. What do they do individually that sets them apart?

### List Several Famous Companies You Know and One Unique Thing about Each One:

*It could be anything like their logo or their company slogan or their packaging or their funny mascot, whatever it may be. Something that makes you remember them.*

# Who Is Your Product or Idea For?

People are your market, this is true. BUT *WHICH* PEOPLE? Men? Women? Kids? Older men? Middle-aged women? Younger kids? Certain ethnic groups?

*WHO? WHO? WHO? WHO? I know I sound like an owl, but you NEED to KNOW THIS ANSWER!*

One great rule of thumb is this: If your product is for EVERYONE, it's usually for NO ONE. It's a very broad brush we use when we say something like: "This is for everyone!" Yes, everyone is the goal, ultimately, but you need to start with a narrower target at the beginning. This will help you focus on a much clearer target. Either start with one customer type or one product. It will make things simpler at the beginning.

When Amazon first started (boy, don't you wish you had invested in that company way back then?!), they shipped ONE product: books. That was it. Why? Because books were easy to ship. They are all the same shape! Different sizes, sure, but the same shape, and they fit into boxes very easily. Once Amazon knew they could do books successfully, then they moved onto other products one by one until they basically took over everything and are now one of the biggest and most successful companies in the world.

Let's look at another product. Something that's used by NEARLY everyone: the iPhone.

The iPhone is owned by millions and millions of people around the world. No doubt about it. BUT it wasn't the iPhone that came first. The iPod came first. And who was the iPod for? People who listened to music. Once the iPod was a proven success, then it was combined with a cell phone to eventually become the iPhone we all know today.

Think about it: A little girl isn't usually going to be interested in something that a 50-year-old woman would be interested in, right? And vice versa. You absolutely need to figure out your target market.

## Who Is Your Product or Idea For?

*List the top 5 options - add more if necessary.*

1.

2.

3.

4.

5.

# What Do People Want?

What do you buy at the market? There are all kinds of things that you buy on a regular basis, right? Things like eggs, bread, cheese, apples, juice, toothpaste—the essentials. Yes, you may spring for a brand-new item or trinket every once in a while, but there are the tried-and-true things that you get every time. Yet, even though you get the essentials, there are certain TYPES of essentials you always get. A certain BRAND. You get that certain brand of toothpaste, that certain brand of cereal, that certain brand of deodorant. But you must ask yourself WHY you get that certain brand. What is it about the brand you buy that makes you keep buying it?

The reason is, more than likely, that it gives you a good feeling. A feeling of comfort and safety. It's those good feelings that keep you coming back over and over again. It's the way our brand will create those good feelings in the customer that will keep them coming back to us.

So, what do people want, and what can you do to help them get it? Outside of family and a few close friends, very few people will buy your product unless they NEED it. Your job, then, as a creative is to figure out HOW you can make people feel that they NEED your product.

But how do we create a product or brand that people will respond to favorably? Is it an instantaneous process? Heck, no! It's like every other process in the world: It takes time. Sometimes, a lot. Sometimes, less, but it takes time, nonetheless. You need time to conceive the product, develop the product, manufacture the product, then advertise and market the product. Do NOT be discouraged when you are moving through this process! It's easy to get that way sometimes as we accomplish and are confronted by task after task after task, but it's the constant "checking off the boxes," the accomplishing the goals, that creates in us the strength to keep going as the goal gets closer and the responsibilities get bigger and bigger.

Think of ways to make your product stand apart from the rest. What makes it something special?

### List Several Ways You Can Make Your Product Stand Out from the Rest:

*Don't freak out if this is hard. Your easiest ideas will come quickly. It's the ones that take time that can sometimes be the best.*

1.

2.

3.

4.

5.

# Section 3: Realization

*I denied myself nothing my eyes desired; I refused my heart no pleasure. My heart took delight in all my labor, and this was the reward for all my toil. Yet when I surveyed all that my hands had done and what I had toiled to achieve, everything was meaningless, a chasing after the wind; nothing was gained under the sun (Ecclesiastes 2:10–11 NIV).*

A word to the reader going forward:

The scripture quoted above was written by King Solomon. This was a man who had everything and more than most people on earth ever dream of. More money, more possessions, more pleasures than anyone could ever even imagine, and yet, when it was all said and done and he wrote this scripture, he told us that all the material gain and earthly goods he acquired over the course of his life was meaningless. It was all "vanity and grasping at the wind."

I say this NOT TO STOP YOU from trying to achieve and grow in your dream—quite the contrary—you NEED TO ACHIEVE YOUR DREAM! And why? Because you need to have ABUNDANCE! Not so you can live a life like Solomon, merely acquiring goods and material objects and pleasures, but so you can BLESS OTHER PEOPLE as you grow and increase.

Solomon was different than you in this way: He did not have Jesus as his Lord and Savior, but YOU DO! You have a greater purpose for your life and your goals than the mere acquisition of material items.

You are a child of the King, and as such, you are either a prince or a princess, and one very great thing princes and princesses can do is make change for the better.

Your purpose is not merely to get here to where you've gotten: to the goal line. Yes, that is the goal and desire at first, but once you get there, then what? Sometimes, it's the "then what?" that can trip us up.

# Here You Are

This section is for the creative Christian that has had, or soon will have, an idea out there in the marketplace that is up and running and is making a profit, no matter how big or how small. If you've developed an idea, and people have paid you money to obtain that product, then this section is for you.

You've overcome the obstacles, you've come through the fire, and here you are: a product on the shelf. Congratulations! It's not been an easy task for sure, and you could probably write a book like this yourself, right? But now that you have something that's been realized, let's take a look at how you can make sure it's always moving in an upward direction. Remember, as a creative Christian, we ALWAYS want to be growing.

As I quoted in an earlier chapter, God told us to "be fruitful and multiply." God is all about multiplication. Even when He subtracts or prunes things in our lives, it's all about multiplication or becoming more fruitful. The only thing Jesus wants us to subtract from our lives are bad behaviors, thoughts, doctrines, and people who are not healthy for us. For everything else—our work, our industry, our goals, our accomplishments, our faith—He wants to grow and prosper.

He says in the book of 3 John 1:2

*Beloved, I pray that you may prosper in all things and be in health, just as your soul prospers.*

So as amazing as it is that your idea is up and running, you want to make sure that it KEEPS running and prospering for as long as possible, right? You want to take as many precautions and plan things out in such a way that your idea—your newfound industry— is viable and thriving even after you leave the earth to go and be with the Lord.

Think about it: You did not work this hard to get things moving to merely have them stop once you're in heaven. There are those coming after you that will greatly benefit from your legacy provided you plan things out properly.

### List Some Ways (or People) That Can Help You Keep Your Dream Going for the Long-Term:

*These ideas may not be easy. But write down what or who comes to mind first.*

1.

2.

3.

4.

5.

Let's look at a few things that a lot of successful business people, especially Christian ones, can implement into their businesses to make them as strong as possible.

# Dedicated unto the Lord

You're a Christian. Jesus is the center of your world, at least He's supposed to be. If you want to see a real hedge of protection around your business and see the Holy Spirit flow through your organization on a daily basis, then be sure to dedicate your work unto Jesus. He will never let you down. He knows how hard you've worked to get here, and He has been with you every step of the way. But take time out of your busy schedule to remember that He is the One who got you here. Without His strength and His love for you—and all the doors of opportunity that He opened for you—you would not be here.

Let me rephrase that: You MIGHT be here, but it would have been a far greater struggle, and once you got to the goal, you'd be full of just as much stress, doubt, and anxiety as the rest of the world.

As Christians, Jesus tells us that we have "overcome the world," meaning, when you dedicate your work to Him, the Lord's favor shines upon you and what is yours.

*Commit to the Lord whatever you do, and he will establish your plans (Proverbs 16:3 NIV).*

New opportunities and avenues for expansion will come, divine connections and meetings will occur. You'll begin to see things work and move in ways that you maybe never thought possible. That's not to say that Jesus is a genie in a bottle. You can't just rub your Bible like rubbing a lamp and expect Jesus to grant you three wishes, but you can gather your team in prayer each morning and pray with them for a successful day. You can lay your hands on your physical work, dedicate it to the Lord, and ask Him to bless it. I have done this countless times with my work over the years, and I have seen God's supernatural abundance and favor shine all over it and bring enormous success.

Now, let me also say this: Dedicating your work to the Lord is not a "one and done" deal. You don't just dedicate your work to the Lord, and *wham!* it's done, and you're instantly a billionaire. No. There will still be obstacles and all kinds of negative things you'll have to overcome as you grow. After all, even though you're a Christian, you are still living in man's world, and man's world is riddled with problems and difficulties. But dedicating your work to the One who died for you— the One who loves you and makes all things possible—is truly something so special and significant that it will most definitely make a huge difference in the way your business grows. Take it from me, I have dedicated all my work to the Lord, and I have seen amazing things happen many, many times.

## How Can We Continue to Dedicate Our Work to the Lord?

1.

2.

3.

# Staying in the Word of God

Yes, Jesus is your Lord and Savior. But how well do you know Him? It is vital that your time with the Lord is not decreased as your success and responsibilities increase. As an entrepreneur, your CEO should be Jesus, plain and simple. He is your rock, He is your fortress, and He is your strong tower. If you get into the weeds with your newfound success and begin to minimize your time with Jesus—if you begin to merely *incorporate* Him when you have some spare time as opposed to *building everything around Him*—you will quickly find yourself living off your own wits and strength, and that will only last so long. After all, how long can you hold 100 pounds over your head without help?

Obtaining the Lord's wisdom is not an easy thing at all. "And why is that?" you may ask. Is Jesus being selfish and not sharing with us? Is He standing, arms folded in defiance with His back to us, refusing to talk to us?

No. Not at all. The secular world is full of all kinds of negative propaganda regarding God, and we are taught from a very young age that God is a punisher and not a friend. We are taught that God is scowling at us constantly and glaring at us with a very judgmental eye. We are taught that we should just forget about God because He has forgotten all about us, but nothing could be further from the truth.

It's not the Lord making it difficult for us to find Him. It is US making it harder than it needs to be! We are the ones who get distracted by the "cares of the world" and the "deceitfulness of riches" (Matthew

13:22). We are the ones who put our attention elsewhere when we should be spending time in our Bibles, listening to Christian teachings, and quieting our spirits as the Lord attempts to provide wisdom and guidance for us. How can we even listen to the Lord's wisdom if we're busy doing everything else with everyone else?

I write this to you not as a person who THINKS it may be a good idea, but as someone who KNOWS firsthand that it's a great idea! As my success in the entertainment business began to grow, I made sure to obtain as much wisdom from the Lord as I could. It wasn't instant, and it certainly wasn't an easy thing to do, but with determination and discipline, I was able to build my business around Him. As the Bible says:

*"Enter by the narrow gate; for wide is the gate and broad is the way that leads to destruction, and there are many who go in by it. Because narrow is the gate and difficult is the way which leads to life, and there are few who find it" (Matthew 7:13–14).*

Some of you may ask me: "Hey, Butch, how did YOU find more wisdom from the Lord? More importantly, how do you CONTINUE to find wisdom?" By reading the Bible on a daily basis and learning more about who Jesus was (and IS), what my authority and duty are as His child, and how to better increase and strengthen my relationship with Him.

Remember the example of Peter: He cast his net when and where Jesus told him to even though his natural (carnal) mind was telling him not to.

Make sure that, no matter what tries to take your time away or distract you, you make an all-out effort to spend as much time with Jesus as possible. Reading, praying, speaking to Him, etc. He is far wiser than any earthly coach you could hire, and He doesn't charge you an hourly rate!

Speaking of hiring an earthly coach....

# A Multitude of Counselors

Whether it's for wisdom for your business, your family, or your finances, gaining wisdom from others who have been there is definitely an asset and not a hindrance, PROVIDED that you do your research and hire the right people. Listen, we live in a "coach-happy" world right now. It seems like everyone on social media these days is a coach of something or other, even though you've probably never heard of them. But there they are, offering you help with money, investing, goal setting, athletics, weight loss, makeup, acting, etc. Finding the right coach for yourself can be a challenge, that's for sure.

One very important note: Do your best to locate a good Christian counselor who practices good, biblical doctrine. The last thing you need is a non-Christian counselor coming in and telling you that all your godly plans and intentions are completely wrong.

A lot of very successful people hire coaches, and yes, they have had to wade through several who didn't work before they found one who did. But the point is that, eventually, they found one who worked for them, and you can, too. Do not feel bad, for one second, that you are thinking about getting counsel for your business, family, or finances. The Bible puts it like this:

*In the multitude of counselors there is safety (Proverbs 11:14).*

In other words, having a lot of knowledgeable people around you is a wise move. None of us know everything, so don't get to a point where pride enters in and says "Well, I got this far on my own. I know I can go a lot farther without help from anyone else." We can only go so far on our own. The bigger you grow and expand, the larger a team and the more counsel you will need. Yes, it's fine to do as much as you can on your own, but finding a highly qualified coach to help counsel you on your future plans can be of great benefit.

My wife and I hired a coach at one point in our careers as our business began expanding. Why did we do this? Because we needed to! We were parents, pastors, and businesspeople who worked with and counseled dozens of people on a weekly basis, and we suddenly realized one day that no one ever counseled us! We needed someone to come in and give us a 3,000-foot view of our lives, worlds, and routines so that we could begin to adjust accordingly. It took a bit of us allowing ourselves to listen and begin to implement some of the ideas and strategies (hey, changing habits and routines is not easy to do, right? Not easy but definitely not impossible!), but once we started making the adjustments our coach suggested, we started noticing a difference in the way we did business and even in the way we did life. Bottom line: It totally helped!

## List the Names of People You Think Would Be Great to Get Advice From...

*Yes, you can list successful people that are well-known if you'd like. Imagine yourself sitting down with them and getting their wisdom firsthand.*

# Legal Stuff

You probably knew this part was coming, and you most likely had two reactions:

1.  You were excited about it.

2.  You were terrified at the very thought of talking about this.

Most people are in the #2 category: terrified to talk about it. But talk about it we must. Legal things are a huge part of the grown-up world, and if you're serious about bringing your vision into a reality, then you are going to have to deal with these things sooner or later. If you learn how to master (or at least begin to understand) the legal system, then you can make it work for you, and things can go much better. If you simply don't want to deal with it, then you are leaving yourself open to a great deal of disappointment and struggle. Trust me, if you don't learn the legalities surrounding your vision, then others will. And if you are not educated, they will take advantage of you. Trust me, there are a great many people out there who do not have your best interests at heart.

## Contracts

We have to talk about this even though, as a creative person, contracts are probably something you really don't look forward to dealing with.

God makes a COVENANT with us but with other people on planet earth we sign a CONTRACT. Why? Well, "God is not a man that He should lie" (Numbers 23:19). This means that GOD ALWAYS TELLS THE TRUTH! When He makes a promise to us—a COVENANT—He keeps it! There is no turning back. He is God, and He must keep His promises. If He were to lie about one thing, then He could lie about many things, and then His Word would be null and void. He could then be discredited like a witness on the stand in a courtroom. God is above reproach, and His Word cannot be discredited.

But we sign contracts with other people because, sometimes, people cannot be trusted to keep their word, and a contract holds them to what was agreed to. Unlike God, people CAN lie, and they do all the time!

This is why contracts are important: to hold people to what they promised to do. As you move forward into your dream becoming a reality, you're going to need to be signing contracts with people who manufacture things, advertise things, sell things—and people who may even end up working for you. You want to make sure that you understand why contracts exist and how they work.

So, how do we go about learning the legalities or the "ins and outs" of the many contracts and pieces of paper we're going to have to look at as we go forward into our vision? Think about it: As you progress and grow, as your idea catches fire and begins to generate income, there are going to be a lot of different avenues you can take to be sure that the income generating process is as smooth as possible.

The first way to learn is simple experience. When I was younger (in my 20s), I was doing some acting work in Hollywood, and when I managed to land an acting job on a show, there would be a contract given to me. On this contract were a ton of words and legal phrases that, quite frankly, scared and confused me. I was a young kid and did NOT know how to read any of this stuff, let alone interpret the meaning behind it all. Followed by all the fancy words was a blank line at the bottom where I was supposed to sign my name and agree to the terms.

Now, at this time, I happened to have an agent who would look over the contract for me. Then— once they were satisfied with the terms—they would advise me to sign it so I could then go and do the acting job. I was very fortunate to have a representative looking out for me, but they didn't do it for free. Oh, heavens no. A good rep or agent will always take a percentage of any money they help to make you (in my case my agent took 10 percent).

*Note: We will talk about the best way to land an agent or representative in the next section, but we are focusing on contracts for now.*

Another way to learn about how contracts work is to ask questions of people who have worked with them. What are some of the pitfalls? What are some of the benefits? What language should be in there, and how many things should or should not be in there? In your journey to get here, you will have undoubtedly run into various people who have dealt with contracts, so take advantage of any relationships you have in the legal area, and ask, ask, ask!

Take classes. Research. Watch instructional YouTube videos. Study, study, study. Remember: You are an adult professional, not an adolescent wannabe. You want to be able to talk the talk and walk the walk.

Remember again: Adults get results.

## List What May Intimidate You about Contracts:

1.

2.

3.

4.

5.

## Getting a Representative (Lawyer or Agent)

"So with all this talk about 'legal' stuff, lawyers, agents, and contracts, how are we supposed to go about actually GETTING an agent, lawyer, or legal representative?" is what you're probably asking, right?

Valid question! These are not just run-of-the-mill folks that we put in our lives on a daily basis. Why is that? Because these individuals are usually people who are paid for their time. And they, quite often, are paid very well. The average lawyer makes upwards of $250–$750 an hour! This depends, of course, on their level of experience and where they are located (a lawyer in New York City, for example, is going to cost a lot more than a lawyer located in, say, Des Moines, Iowa), but there is always—usually— an expense when it comes to legal counsel. But remember: This is serious business. This is YOUR business, and it is a cost that you will need to prepare for. If this makes you nervous or scares you, please don't worry. As you move down the road toward your goal, you'll see how necessary this expense is, and you'll find the funding for it somehow. Look at it this way: When your small, home-grown peanut butter company begins to get noticed by a national supermarket chain, and they want to make you an offer, do you feel confident negotiating that deal yourself?

Exactly. You need wisdom around you. As much wisdom as possible.

Who is going to speak for you? I know, I know, you're probably thinking, *I can speak for myself, and no one is ever going to take that away from me!*

I know.

But when I say, "speak for you," I don't necessarily mean *talking,* like just sitting and talking to someone else and running your company and managing your idea.

What I really mean is who is going to *negotiate* for you?

Yes. The art of negotiation. There's a reason it's called an art. Because not everyone is good at it! You may be good at the skill or ability you are currently trying to market—like designing clothes for toddlers or making unicycles for frogs—but once the opportunity comes and someone wants to finance your project and help to make it a reality, then the question remains:

Who is going to negotiate that for you?

*This bears repeating:*

*But in the multitude of counselors there is safety (Proverbs 11:14).*

As we're starting out, the "counselors" we have around us are usually our friends and immediate family. They all pour their thoughts and life experiences into us and try their best to give us their thoughts on each and every situation. But as we get farther down the road toward our dream, we need to get counsel from those who already work or have worked in our chosen field. It's just common sense.

When a young boy first starts out playing baseball, his first coach is usually his own father. The father is the closest one to the boy at that point in his life, and the young boy will be coached to the extent of the father's wisdom. But as the boy progresses and becomes a better, higher-level player, he will need a better, higher-level coach. One that most likely knows more about the sport than his father does. This is a big moment for the boy AND the father as they each must come to terms with the fact that the boy will now be coached by someone else who will better benefit the boy.

What if the boy and father refused to get new coaching because they were afraid to trust someone else? Wouldn't that be greatly limiting for the boy's baseball career? See how a fearful attitude could greatly hinder the potential career of the boy simply because both the boy and his father were fearful about trusting someone else?

I had to learn this about my own career. I was good at drawing but not so good at negotiating. Had I tried to negotiate deals myself—with no training—I would have greatly hindered my own career.

If you're in the entertainment business, like I am, you need a good entertainment lawyer. This is just what it sounds like: a lawyer that specializes in entertainment. This is someone who knows the ins and outs of the business and can help you craft the best deal possible.

Each area of manufacturing or whatever business you happen to be in usually has law experts that specialize in that area. You should be able to find a good one once you're ready to find one. A lawyer will usually get paid in one of two ways:

1. They will charge an hourly rate.

2. They will take a small percentage of the final deal.

The hourly rate option is good because you pay them, and then it's done. But this may be a very big expense for you up front.

The percentage option is also good because you pay nothing up front; HOWEVER, the lawyer gets a percentage of the final deal for life. FOR LIFE! The percentage is usually 3 percent–5 percent, so it's not much, but you need to take this into consideration. Listen: Everyone needs to get paid, including you. But these types of expenses are going to become commonplace as you begin to build your dream.

Now, if you're going to get an AGENT—which is someone who helps you get connections and meetings and can negotiate deals for you—you need to remember several things:

1.  An agent is NOT a legal representative. They know their way around a contract for sure, but they are not a lawyer.

2.  An agent, customarily, will take 10 percent of any deal that comes in—for the LIFE of the project.

You might be a bit concerned about the 10 percent and the life of the project talk, but this is how a lot of deals are done. You can negotiate any terms with your representative that you're able to, but the terms I laid out earlier are usually customary. For me, I'd rather pay a good representative a small percentage and keep up to 90 percent, than try to negotiate the deal myself and lose even more percentage by not knowing the ins and outs and what I could have asked for. If you don't know how to negotiate a contract, you will lose more than you can make because you will not understand the terminology. For me, I don't want to screw things up, so I look at hiring a qualified, hard-working representative as definitely a price worth paying.

"And how do I find an agent or manager, Butch?" you're asking. This is definitely something that you have to learn. It's not super difficult, but it is something you may not be used to doing.

Lawyers are simpler to find. You can make a phone call or send an email, and a lawyer will most likely get back in touch with you. They won't instantly work with you, and you will have to explain your goals and such, but you can at least get in touch with one more quickly than an agent.

Now, an agent is a different story. Agents are far more exclusive than lawyers, and the only way they will take you on and represent you is if they realize they can make money from you. That may sound harsh, but once they DO agree to represent you, they will be able to get you meetings and connections you would never have been able to get on your own. Having an agent is like having another version of yourself out there working the phones while you spend time working on your product.

One good way to obtain an agent is to check them out online and see how they look for new clients to represent. Go to seminars, go to meet-and-greets. Get out there and meet people! Or, find someone else who has an agent and get them to refer you. I got my first agent by a friend referring me to them, but once I had that referral, it was up to me to prove that I was worth it. I had to show the agent that I could make them money, and in return, they could make me money as well.

There are many different ways and tactics you can employ to find a quality representative, but in the end, they will be an asset to you. Just begin to get used to the idea that you can find one and that you DESERVE to find one. Your idea is great and needs to be represented properly! There is an old saying: "He who represents himself has a fool for a client." I'm not saying that I agree with this saying 100 percent, but I do agree that, most of the time, if we go into something with not as much knowledge as we should have, we are definitely walking on thin ice.

### List Some Steps You Will Now Take to Get an Agent or Lawyer:

1.

2.

3.

4.

5.

# Team Building

Why do you need a team? Why is this important? Aren't you doing great on your own and don't need anyone else? Have you been burned numerous times and would rather go it alone, sink or swim?

Let me just tell you something: Answering yes to the last question is planning for disaster.

Why? Simple: because, by this point, I think you've realized that you cannot do this by yourself. Any endeavor—anything worth building—takes time and takes people to help. From a skyscraper to an outhouse, a team is necessary for expansion, and you'll need to build a team around yourself if you're going to expand and grow your dream into a reality. The reason? Because, try as you might, you simply can't be everywhere at once. You will need others to be where you can't and to also think of ideas you can't.

How easy has it been doing it all by yourself so far? I'm sure you're creative and hard-working and motivated and incredibly adaptable, but the bottom line is that YOU'RE LIMITED. All human beings are, and this is why we need a savior in the form of our Lord Jesus. He is unlimited, and when we dedicate our work to Him, then we instantly acquire His strength and wisdom. And the very first thing He will tell us is to give some of the work to others, so we don't shoulder it all ourselves. Think of it: If you do it all, you will not only be exhausted, but you'll miss doing certain things because there simply isn't time.

However, by allowing others to take part, use their talents, and grow in their skills, then not only are you building a goal, but you're building and training an army of folks that will begin to excel and take pride in the work that they do. A great team can accomplish much more than one person can, which is why it is imperative for you to learn to be involved with others. Being alone is what the enemy wants. If you're alone, you're vulnerable. There's a scripture that covers this:

*Be sober, be vigilant; because your adversary the devil walks about like a roaring lion, seeking whom he may devour (1 Peter 5:8).*

The scripture says that devil "walks about like a roaring lion." A lion is a hunter, and it is constantly looking for something to devour. Will it try to devour the prey that's in a group and protected by others?

No. It is always going to go for the prey that's alone. Solitary. Unprotected. The one that's the most vulnerable. A vulnerable individual is the one the enemy will always go for first because, like the lion, the devil does NOT want to work hard. He is a lazy, uncreative enemy, but like any enemy, he is always looking to hurt someone, especially you.

As a Christian, as a creative person, as a team leader, you need to know how to resist the devil. Yes, RESIST. You are capable of resisting him, and you can do it with practice and determination. Just like all the other things we've talked about in this book, it will take you being determined and disciplined in learning how to do it. But we must remember to not be afraid to resist. Sometimes, we get so used to taking what the world gives us that we forget we have the ability to change anything. We MUST remember that it is

WE who are in control of our lives and not the world. Your team will be a reflection of who you are, and if you want a great team, you must become as great a leader as possible. It won't happen overnight, and you'll need to constantly adjust as you go, but it only happens if you want it to happen.

Remember: All of this only happens if you want it. Do you? You can't do it all alone.

## Your Light and Influence

So why are you doing this? Is it money? Fame? Self-glory? Or is there a higher purpose to all of your actions? Obviously, there should be a higher purpose; otherwise, there really isn't much point in doing it at all. If this venture/dream/goal is only going to serve you and you alone, then you may as well not do it.

Why? Because anyone can do something temporary. Happens every day. But you ... you're different. You are an eternal being. A spiritual being. A being who can influence GENERATIONS if you want to. Getting your bills paid is one thing. Changing lives, cultures, and the world is another. You really need to ask yourself this question: Why? Once you've reached a certain level or goal, you need to ask yourself, "Was this the purpose? Simply to reach this goal?"

Or was there something more? Your heart knows the truth, and the truth is that, yes, you are wanting to build something more than a simple system that pays the bills. You have, in your power, to build something most people can only dream of:

A LEGACY.

# Your Legacy

The Bible is over 2,000 years old. We're able to read and experience it because people took the time to write it down for us. Thank God, they did! If it were not for them, we would never have been able to experience the love of Jesus because we most likely never would have known about Him. The same goes for you!

Who is going to carry on your legacy after you've gone?

Who will make sure your vision continues long after you've entered Heaven? We all know as Christians that Heaven is the ultimate goal, of course, but there will be others who come after us on the Earth who can greatly benefit from the things we leave behind. As you've read in this book, I stress the importance of fellowship, of team building, and the importance of family. The reason for this is because God also sees them as important. A family, a team, a collection of people who can help tell your story and dream to the world is something that can be incredibly important. Even Jesus had disciples that were able to tell His story to the world! If we isolate ourselves and never interact with people, then we end up doing ourselves a disservice. But, sometimes, interacting with others can be very intimidating for people, and we'd just as soon avoid it because it seems more comfortable. But guess what? Getting uncomfortable is exactly what we need to do if we're going to leave a positive legacy of any kind at all.

Think about it: You're going to end up leaving a legacy behind no matter what. Think about that.

Each and every one of us leaves our thumbprint on this world simply by virtue of having had a life here. You have impacted and will continue to impact people in either a positive or negative way no matter what. The question you should ask yourself is: "How do I want to be remembered?"

That's a big question, isn't it? You may say, "I don't care how I'm remembered. I won't be here, so who cares?"

My question for you is: Who benefits from your life? Who HAS benefited from your life? Has your life been a positive experience for those around you, or have you created negative experiences?

Are you being tolerated or are you being appreciated? As a Christian creative, it's your job to understand one of the greatest powers that you have: the POWER OF INFLUENCE.

Your light and influence will affect a great many people during the course of your lifetime, but the most important thing you need to learn is *how* you're going to affect them. Will it be positive or negative? Light or shadow? Which world will you invite people into?

You need to take this seriously. Your dream—your creation, your goal— will affect others long after you've gone. You must be incredibly aware of the importance of the influence you carry. That's the problem with the corruption that has permeated the world over the years. So many of us have become distracted and defeated that we're sometimes unaware we even carry a responsibility in the first place. But God tells us that we have a purpose:

*Great are your purposes and mighty are your deeds. Your eyes are open to the ways of all mankind; you reward each person according to their conduct and as their deeds deserve (Jeremiah 32:19).*

It's up to us to fulfill our purpose. If we choose to not follow our purpose—if we continue to blame others for our problems—then we'll miss out on the incredible experiences that come from embracing the enjoyment of life and learning through the different experiences we'll gather as we move forward. Harness any fear that tries to creep in and take control of your thoughts. The Bible says in 2 Corinthians 10:5, "bringing every thought into captivity to the obedience of Christ...." Let's think logically: If it says to "bring every thought into captivity," that must mean it's our choice whether we want to bring it into captivity or not.

Our choice.

Make the correct choice and take captive the thoughts of fear and defeat. Your purpose is too important to let anything else get in the way of what God has prepared for you. If you want to walk in freedom, you'll have to fight for it. Freedom is never free. It will always cost something. Jesus paid a high price for our freedom, and the least we can do for Him is to take advantage of what He paid for.

## One More Thing: You Don't Always Have to Make Bible Stories!

Let's talk about being a Christian creative. A lot of us feel as though, since we love Jesus and that He is our Lord and Savior, we ALWAYS have to make sure that each and every story we tell is Bible-based.

That we have to include the Scripture, mention biblical characters and themes, and invite people to receive Jesus into their hearts.

Now, I am NOT saying to NOT do those things. Those things are awesome and amazing, and if you can include them, then by all means do. But there are so many stories inside of us that simply may not be able to support including every one of those ingredients. For example, you may want to tell a detective story. A science fiction story. A fantasy story. A romantic comedy. Whatever the story is, it's okay to make it your own. Just make sure it's a narrative that's compelling, engaging, entertaining, and exalts God in some way.

A lot of jobs in the entertainment industry simply don't allow any sort of mention of religion or relationship with Jesus in any way. But that's okay. Your Heavenly Father knows you must work. He also knows what your hopes and dreams are, and He's known them your entire life.  He knows that the job you've always wanted may be in an industry where you must be "as wise as a serpent and as harmless as a dove," and He knows that it may not be favorable to mention His name in the work you do. This doesn't mean that Jesus wants you to lose your job or that He even wants you to feel bad. But what He DOES want is your heart. He wants all the work you do to be done for Him, no matter what.

*And whatever you do, do it heartily, as to the Lord and not to men, knowing that from the Lord you will receive the reward of the inheritance; for you serve the Lord Christ (Colossians 3:23–24)*

Now, having said all that, my advice is this: If you are a child of the Most High God, if you're a follower of Jesus Christ and want to glorify Him in everything you do, then you'll find a way to glorify your King in all the work you produce, no matter what it is. Maybe you've written an animated show. A sports movie, a spy thriller, whatever. That's great! Is there a way you could possibly include some redemptive elements in the story? Maybe you aren't going to be able to mention His name openly (believe me, He's used to that), but the principles and teachings of Jesus can be infused into whatever you do. Principles like love, joy, happiness, forgiveness, loving your neighbor as yourself. A lot of modern audiences won't watch an openly Bible-based story, but they will watch modern stories about current events and situations they can relate to.

Including the teachings of our Lord into our work is beneficial to both you and the audience you're trying to reach. Everyone benefits when Jesus is in the mix.

# Conclusion: Looking Forward

So where do you go from here?

Easy: the place you've always wanted to go—forward. You've been able to look at a great many things by reading this book: your reasons why, your strengths, your weaknesses, your potential team members, legal things, etc. Consider this book a checklist of sorts for the journey you're on. Use it as a reference guide for those times you're not sure of what to do next or who to do it with. Use it to take stock of where you're currently positioned on your journey and what to look at as you take your next step.

This book was not intended to be a "one and done," meaning don't just read it once and put it aside. Use it to strengthen your resolve and further your thinking and planning. After all, there's an old saying that says, "If you fail to plan, you plan to fail." Don't rush. Trust me on this one. Rushing will only rush you into the failure you've been trying to avoid.

(Every time we rush something we get an Ishmael. Read the story in Genesis 16.)

But don't take forever to get going either. Take risks. Be bold. Be brave. It's the courageous ones who stand a better chance of winning because they won't stop when obstacles present themselves. Yes, becoming courageous takes work, sometimes a lot of it. But what else would you be doing if you weren't pursuing your dream with everything you have?

I want you to win. You want you to win. Most importantly, Jesus wants you to win. Let's get going.

God bless.

--Butch

Made in the USA
Las Vegas, NV
18 December 2024

14895317R00095